PRAUS

PRAUS

A Parable for Winning the War Within

Hunter Lambeth

Dedication

For Tommy, my beloved blood brother, whose life was cut far too short and much too early. Without consciously intending to do so, he practiced many of the virtues expounded upon in this book. You are missed every day, "T Bird," every...single...day.

Praus

[prah-oos]

Greek, adj. Mild, gentle, related to but not fully synonymous with meek; demonstrating power without undue harshness; strength under control.

A military term in ancient Greece used to describe the resolute focus and discipline of a powerful war horse, trained to obey every command of its rider, no matter how great the confusion of battle.

Table of Contents

Author's Note. xi

The Clearing xv

Chapter 1   Jerry 1

Chapter 2   The Island 14

Chapter 3   Capsized. 19

Chapter 4   Man In the Mirror 26

Chapter 5   Back to Katherine 51

Chapter 6   Back to the Island. 60

Chapter 7   *Praus* 73

Chapter 8   The Dance 83

Chapter 9   On the Water 100

Chapter 10   The Stones. 113

Chapter 11   Tom 125

Chapter 12   Atlanta 129

Chapter 13   Frozen Again 147

Chapter 14   Chicago 156

Postscript 171

About the Author. 177

Author's Note

In a way the timing was completely coincidental. Sure, I had known my *de facto* mentor David Harper for nearly ten years when he shared with me the short manuscript he had recently completed. Written for a modern audience, *The Great 8: A New Paradigm for Leadership* centered around an ancient event that took place in the Middle East, a world away from the Atlanta suburbs where David and I first met through a mutual friend and where we saw each other almost weekly before I moved my family across the globe. Who could have imagined that at the time I received David's manuscript I would be living about a half hour's drive from the very site of that ancient event?

An avid cyclist, I once a week found myself riding just beneath a bluff where the event in question took place. On that day, several thousand years earlier, a simple man from a nearby village spoke to a hungry people. Opposite the bluff then, and still gurgling in the distance now, is a natural spring and beyond it a shimmering lake. All those many centuries ago the man surveyed a large gathering of people on the hillside above the bluff. He spoke for some time about many things, his voice carrying up, out and over the throng of listening humanity. Finally, no doubt tired and with his throat likely strained from speaking, he left them to contemplate the significance of his message. In particular their thoughts remained upon eight simple and yet profound truths of which he had spoken.

As they watched him go, the audience pondered these truths, the very same ones that would form the foundation of David Harper's treatise some two thousand years later. Designed originally to address the challenges facing the modern businessman or woman, these "Great 8" truths, as David labeled them, actually form a foundation for living in general. David's conviction closely followed the implication that was clear that day long ago on the hillside: these eight simple virtues are the keys to finding peace and harmony within oneself as well as between genders, cultures, and nations.

I pulled my bike over to the side of the road and stood staring across the lake. In ancient times many of the locals referred to the lake as a sea. I looked north and east across the body of water. Not much more than an hour's drive from where I stood lies the border of Syria, a country embroiled in the fourth year of a tragic civil war that has resulted in the displacement of some two million refugees. Not long ago I visited some of those refugees in Jordan where whole families labor through each day just over the hills I could see from my vantage point above the sea. Further east the nation of Iraq is unraveling almost daily at the hands of ISIS, perhaps the most evil and barbaric group the world has seen since the Holocaust. Beyond Baghdad lies the empire of Iran, which some believe is champing at the bit to obliterate the very soil on which I now stood. Letting my gaze drift down across the sea to the south, I considered Egypt, which has been dipping in and out of political, social, and economic upheaval for nearly half a decade now. Even the country where I currently live, the nation state of Israel, is continually at odds, often violently, with its geographic neighbor and Semitic cousin Palestine. I spend time in both places on a weekly basis, maintaining residence in Israel but frequently visiting friends and co-workers in the West Bank. On both sides of this divide I have discovered a vast majority who want to find a way to put aside their differences and live in peace but instead keep seeing that dream derailed by a radicalized minority.

I stood beside my bike, overlooking the waters of the lake-sea, and recalled that day long ago when the simple man shared simple truths on the hillside behind me. How tragic it would be if it were no longer possible to capture their essence and attempt to live by them. I did not want to accept that possibility. Then another thought entered my mind. In light of all the suffering, injustice, and oppression in the region where I stood that day, it occurred to me that perhaps those eight simple yet profound principles might be the modern world's *only* hope. Our greatest minds, our most accomplished academics, and our leading politicians continually seem to come up miserably short in solving the conflicts that plague us. Perhaps, just perhaps, what we need instead is a return to the timeless principles of the ancient world. Might it be there, in the words of the simple man, that we find the strength needed to face the issues of the day and overcome them?

The book you hold in your hands is both an amplification of David Harper's brilliant piece as well as a deeper look into our individual battles with life's inevitable psychological roadblocks. Though based on the words first spoken on that hillside in the heart of the Middle East, the context is different. The time is now. The characters are from a culture that we know well, perhaps too well. Yet the truths continue to stand as guides for unlocking the secrets of life since at its core those things do not change nearly as much as we sometimes think, despite the evidence that at times seems to scream to the contrary.

The story you are about to begin is based on David's attempt to apply those truths to the daily challenges we face in our modern world. My words build upon his. Listen to them; digest them; challenge their validity if you must; but don't ignore them. There is too much at stake. And if you focus, if you really pay attention and approach the text with an open mind, you just might hear the echo of that ancient spring bubbling up and tumbling down the hillside into the sea.

Hunter Lambeth
Northern Galilee, Israel
May, 2015

The Clearing

I pushed my way through the last stand of brush before the jungle cleared and I stood on the edge of a small meadow. At the other end of the clearing was a modest bungalow, oddly eight-sided and seemingly out of place here in the middle of nowhere, yet for a reason I couldn't explain the feeling I had was one of peace, not fear.

The sun was dropping rapidly now, and dusk was beginning to settle around the island. Through a window I could see a light inside the small house. I crossed the meadow and stood at the door of the bungalow. I breathed deeply and knocked. After a few minutes I started to knock again before noticing that the door was slightly open, just enough to betray the light I had seen from the edge of the trees. I pushed the door wide open. The light came from a reading lamp sitting atop an end table positioned beside a large, comfortable-looking reading chair. The rest of the room was bathed in the half-light of dusk.

"Hello," I said. "Is anyone here? I'm lost and need some help."

No response. I waited a moment more and then stepped slowly inside. There was a small kitchen to my left. A teapot rested on the stove, and I could see steam coming from it. Beyond the kitchen was another door leading perhaps to a bedroom. I called toward it, "Hello? My name is Jack. I'm lost, and I just need to use a phone. Don't mean to bother anyone. I just need some help." Still, only silence.

I slowly stepped across the room toward the chair. On a coffee table in front of it was a large leather-bound book opened in the middle. Beside the book was a cup of what looked to be tea, newly brewed, the steam still wafting up. There were fresh stains on one of the pages. It seemed that whoever had been reading had accidentally spilled some of the hot tea on the book.

I leaned over the table, momentarily forgetful of my circumstances and curious about the book. Because of the angle, I had to strain my neck to see what was written on the stained pages.

"Well, hello there." A voice behind me pierced the silence, and I whirled around, ready to explain or defend myself, whatever the moment might demand. In the process I hit the table, and the cup of hot tea spilled completely over.

"Well, guess I'll need more towels," said the voice. "Looks like you've finished what I began."

The voice was that of an old man, at least twenty-five years my senior, maybe more. He wore blue jeans and sneakers with a T-shirt underneath a thin fleece pullover. I was struck by the thought that he dresses a lot like I do when I'm loafing around the house. Apparently he had become chilly in the afternoon storm. That explained the hot tea on a tropical island.

"Don't worry," he said. "You didn't startle me. I heard you when you came in. I was just too preoccupied to answer, looking for a towel to clean up my spill."

"You startled *me*," I said.

He started to walk over to where I stood by the desk. "Let me get that before it soaks in any further."

"Oh," I said, apologetically. "Yeah, I'm really sorry about that."

"Not to worry, son, " he said. In my late fifties it felt odd to be called "son" by anyone other than my own father.

The old man came close, and as he passed our eyes met and I recoiled. My knees grew a little weak, and I had to reach out for the chair to steady myself. Suddenly I realized why he dressed like me.

"You, you . . . ," I stammered, completely undone by what I now saw in his face.

"I know, " he said nonchalantly. "It seems really strange at first."

"You . . . you look just like *me*! Or at least an older version of me," I added.

"Yeah, but there's a good reason for that."

"A good reason?"

"Yes," he said, "because . . . ."

I cut him off. "Because why?"

"Because, Jack, I *am* you."

Jerry

To begin with, the horse was imposing to gaze upon. He was a destrier, known for being the finest of battle horses, though not always of correct temperament. Naturally powerful, he was impressive to take in, even from a distance. When last measured he was said to stand more than eighteen hands high, meaning even a man of six feet would only be his equal at the wither along his shoulder blades. But nearly a year had passed since anyone had taken the time to calculate the horse's height, and the men who attended to him now were far too busy with more important things than taking updated measurements. Determining any change in his height had fallen down the list of priorities. Instead the great beast watched from the shadows of his stall as the men in camp rose early and slept little and busied themselves endlessly sharpening tools, stockpiling weapons, and readying for the now inevitable situation that had been thrust upon them. War.

A friend of mine once told me that every businessman will have his "Jerry McGuire moment." You remember the movie, don't you? Sports agent Jerry wakes up sweating in the middle of the night, deeply troubled that his firm has become more concerned with the bottom dollar at the expense of the human element that brought in the firm's clients. He pounds out a manifesto, a personal "mission statement" he calls it. The words and ideas are celebrated by his colleagues, but Jerry is promptly fired the following week since his personal revelation is seen as a threat to the bottom dollar. He strikes out on his own, taking one idealistic secretary with him, and eventually realizes his heartfelt ideals and convictions. He builds a firm based on those principles, things like honesty, integrity, compassion, and relational transparency.

My friend told me that, while everyone will eventually have his or her McGuire moment, it's how you respond to that moment that matters. Most of us don't have the guts to do what Jerry did. We don't have the financial leverage, the personal or emotional security, or the courage to take such a risk, placing our immediate and future standing so far out on a limb.

I finally met Jerry a couple of years ago. He showed up unexpectedly in the middle of a very typical, routine, and, sadly, disappointing business seminar. I had flown up to Chicago for the event. By this time, having logged decades in the corporate world and having attended hundreds of such gatherings, I should have known better, but I boarded the plane with a refreshed sense of hope. *Maybe this would be the exception,* I coached myself. *Maybe this would be the moment when I would leave such an event motivated and equipped with helpful new insights for the immediate future.*

It was mid-winter. Chicago was covered by snow and ice. I was hoping for some inspiration to take back with me to Georgia. What I received instead was actually *de-motivating.* I did gain insight, but not the kind I had expected.

All of the attendees, including those from our firm, were in the executive-benefits business together through a joint marketing agreement. The leader of our contingent, who happened to be the featured speaker for the final morning's session, had the reputation of being a real superstar in our business. At first we were enamored by his mystique. We viewed him as the epitome of success. Whenever we brought him into client situations, people were always impressed. But over time small inconsistencies between what was being promised and what we could deliver had begun to appear. It had taken a while before it became clear that our values were much different than our leader's, as well as those of most of the other people in the group.

He was driven by ego and selfish ambition. I got the distinct impression that almost everything he said was intended to create an inflated picture of himself. Yet, for some strange reason, I and others in our firm had fallen into a pattern of placating this particular exec by stroking his ego. In retrospect, I cannot believe we put up with this behavior as long as we did. The Chicago seminar was several years into the work relationship, and he made the statement that he and several other attendees were the "A Team" and that we should bring them in on all of our new business opportunities. It was like being kicked in the gut. The implication was that the rest of us were the "B Team." I wondered why they considered themselves the "A Team." Some of them consistently produced less than we did, yet they dominated most of the discussion, and they seemed to enjoy hearing themselves talk while the rest of us sat in silence, not voicing our objections.

Suddenly I felt a presence lurking just over my left shoulder. I glanced up. There he was, smiling down at me and nodding as if to say he knew exactly what I was thinking. I had come face to face with my Jerry McGuire. I felt frozen in place and paralyzed. This was it, just as my friend had warned. Jerry had come to visit me. I looked back toward the stage at Mr. A Team. I tried to ignore the image of Tom Cruise, the actor who played Jerry in the movie, but I could feel him lurking in the space just above my shoulder, wondering what I was going to do.

As I tried hard to block out Jerry and listen to Mr. A Team, the inevitable wasn't hard to imagine. There was no doubt in my mind that it would be only a matter of time before all the guys on the ego-driven "A Team" would be at each other's financial throats, suing each other and doing everything they could to create separation and cutthroat competition. Maybe being relegated to the "B Team" had its advantages after all.

But at that moment, with Jerry hanging over my shoulder and Mr. A Team narcissistically waxing poetic on the stage, I couldn't say with any certainty whether I'd be on *any* team in the near future.

Jerry was egging me on. *You know this isn't right*, he whispered. I turned away, glancing toward the other half of the room. *You know this isn't what you signed up for all those years ago. This isn't what you believe in. This isn't what you have worked so hard to be a part of. This isn't right.*

Leave me alone, I replied.

I can't.

Why?

Because this isn't me talking. This is YOU talking.

I shuddered. He was right. And at that moment so many things I had been seeing and feeling and wrestling with for years came crashing into focus. I realized that the whole issue of values was even bigger and more important to me than I had been willing to believe. And the time had come when I, along with others around me, had to clarify for our strategic partners, our clients, and ourselves what that gap really meant for us both personally and professionally.

Mr. A Team was talking. I could see his mouth moving, but I couldn't anymore hear a word he was saying. I was far away now, lost in contemplation. Jerry was no longer behind my shoulder but rather staring me square in the face. He was demanding a decision on my part, some course of action. I felt as if I were looking in a mirror. Some place deep within me was struggling to be bold and courageous about convictions that had long been suppressed.

A day later I was on the plane home to Atlanta, barely aware of what I had done in the hours since that fateful encounter. I know that I went to dinner with co-workers at a downtown Chicago restaurant. I know that I watched a late-night ESPN broadcast lying in my hotel bed. I recall talking to my wife Katherine on the phone for a few minutes before I went to sleep. She kept asking me what was wrong, sensing something in my voice, but I couldn't answer. It wasn't that I was avoiding the question. I was just unsure of myself, maybe for the first time in my adult life, and I couldn't give her a clear answer.

The plane leveled off, and the flight attendants started the beverage service. When the attendant in our cabin leaned over to ask me what I wanted to drink, he had to repeat the question three times before I heard him. I had been staring out the window and searching the clouds for Jerry McGuire. He was nowhere to be found.

———

The next morning, a Saturday, I awoke unmotivated and uninspired. It took every ounce of discipline I could muster to pull myself from bed, shower, dress, and make my way to the kitchen. This was strange for me. Normally I was a morning person. I liked to be up just before sunrise, coffee in one hand and a book in the other, treading quietly so as not to wake Katherine, and make my way to my favorite reading chair in the den. But on this particular morning, an especially cold one even by Georgia standards, I felt like a sloth.

I sat down in our breakfast nook, and Katherine poured me a cup of strong coffee. She started to add my normal dose of cream and sugar, but I stopped her.

"Not this morning, I said. "I need it as black and strong as possible."

She looked at me with pity and sighed. "Talk to me, Jack," she said in her soothing way. "Just if you want to. If it will help."

She knew about my struggles and frustrations at work. Beyond being a remarkable wife, Katherine was a gifted interpreter of thoughts and feelings, as well as a patient listener, a willing sounding board when I needed that. So I returned her sigh and launched into my story. I told her about my time in Chicago, about the less than inspiring speakers, the dull seminars, the redundant, regurgitated information that had grown old for me. I told her how such seminars seemed like nothing more than an annual formality. And then I told her about my encounter with Jerry McGuire. Katherine and I had seen the movie together some fifteen years earlier, and she remembered it even better than I.

"Honey," I said, "it was almost as though there really was someone there right behind me in that room and talking directly to me."

"I wonder what it all means? " she replied.

Katherine was always ready to look more deeply below the surface than I was. She didn't want to waste much time on the trivial or irrelevant. She wanted to dig and probe and get to the roots of the issue.

"I don't know, " I said despondently. "That's what I'm trying to figure out. But right now . . . well, right now I feel more confused than anything. Maybe even a little depressed."

She reached across the table and put her hand over mine.

"I kind of feel as if, well, I've lost my way a little bit," I added, staring into my coffee. "I mean, the reasons I got into this kind of work in the first place . . . all those years of training and investing and learning and then imparting what I learned to others . . . all those long days, the extra hours, the trips away from you and the kids . . . sometimes. . . ." My voice trailed off.

"What is it Jack?" Katherine's soft voice brought me back.

"Sometimes I wonder it it's all been worth it."

Katherine straightened up. "Listen to me, Jack Harper, love of my life. Don't you for one minute question the path you've taken to this point. You have built a great life. You have raised a great family—three remarkable kids and, in turn, four of the most precious grandchildren anyone could hope for. You have worked hard and. . . ."

"Geez, Katherine," I interrupted. "You make it sound as though I'm accepting some kind of award or something. I have plenty of faults, you know."

She nodded and squeezed my hand. "I do know that about you. I know everything about you, and I. . . ."

My cell phone rang where it lay on the table in front of me. I looked down to see who the caller was. It was my closest business partner and one of my best friends, Tom. He had been with me in Chicago.

"That can wait, " Katherine said. "I want to finish my thought here."

I hit the decline button, but a moment later the phone rang again. I reached for it.

"*Jack*," Katherine warned me.

"Honey, I really appreciate what you are saying, but I need to take this call. It's Tom. He's probably sitting at the table with Beth right now having this same discussion. He came back from Chicago pretty much down in the dumps right along with me."

Probably feeling sorry for me and knowing a word from Tom might cheer me up, Katherine relented. "It's fine. Really. Go ahead," she said and stood to refill her coffee mug.

Tom and I spoke for a few seconds before I closed the phone, took a last sip of coffee, and stood up from the table. I went to Katherine, looked her in the eyes, and told her I loved her. Kissed her, I then hurriedly left the kitchen.

"Wait a minute," she called after me. "Where are you going? I was just getting ready to make you an awe-inspiring, spirits-lifting, Southern breakfast."

"To meet Tom," I answered over my shoulder. "Starbucks."

"What? Is my coffee not black and strong enough for you?" she said, trying to lighten what had been a somber beginning to the day.

"Your coffee is the best. Your breakfasts are the best. I just need to spend some time talking this out with Tom."

I grabbed my fleece pullover and my car keys and opened the front door. As I was pulling the door closed behind me, I heard Katherine yelling from the kitchen. "Listen, I have a great idea. I think we should. . . ."

The door shut out her words, and I felt a wave of guilt come over me. I know that she had been trying to help me in the way only she could, but Tom had sounded especially disturbed on the phone, almost panicked. I backed out of the driveway and broke a few speeding limits on my way to my usual Starbucks.

———

Tom was there waiting for me, almost hidden back in the only shadowy corner of the coffee shop. He'd already ordered a strong double-shot espresso and was nervously rubbing his hands around the cup. I couldn't tell whether he was trying to get warm or having some kind of mini emotional breakdown. It turned out that it was a little of both.

"Go ahead and order, he said, looking up. "I didn't want to take a chance of missing out on this table."

"Actually, I'm pretty awake now," I said and sat down opposite him. "Didn't sleep well at all."

"Jack," he said, looking up at me. "What are we going to do?"

I nodded. "Yeah, what *are* we gonna do?"

There was a long pause, and the question hung in the air like the unmistakable smell of recently roasted coffee beans. Tom looked okay this morning, but the truth was that he was battling an aggressive cancer. He was nearly a year into his war against the disease, already accustomed to chemo sessions and radiation treatments and days when he couldn't make it out of bed and into the office.

I and others had strongly advised him against attending the Chicago seminar, but he had insisted, and I could see now that the trip had worn him out both physically and emotionally. Anyone would have forgiven him if he decided to step completely away from work, abandon his ongoing battle against what he perceived to be the death of ethical business, and just spend his days with his family and golf clubs. But he had too much pride and determination for that. Like myself, Tom had invested so much of his life in building a strong, reputable business résumé, and he wasn't willing to let it go just because others had lost their way. And he certainly wasn't going to give cancer the upper hand by surrendering his work ethic. Indeed, over the last several years Tom and I had worked hand in hand trying to encourage a new business standard, only to be beaten down and discouraged by the willingness of others around us to compromise ethics and principles for the sake of the bottom dollar. Chicago had merely been the latest for both of us in a long line of bitter reality checks.

"I don't know," Tom said, a look of heavy anxiety on his face, "but I don't think I can keep going with the way things are. I mean, we're getting older. We should be hitting our stride about now and seeing our ultimate business dreams realized, but I feel as though we're heading in the opposite direction. Sometimes . . . well, sometimes I feel that we're losing sight of our dreams."

"Or having them pulled out from under us," I offered.

"It's not fair to us and, more importantly perhaps, it's not fair to the clients who trust us. I mean, it's almost unethical."

With a knowing glance, we both instantly thought of several things to which Tom was referring. We had strategic partners who were constantly making promises to clients, some of them quite significant, and then failing to deliver altogether. Or, at best, making promises and then delaying making good on them, to the point that the clients were frustrated and our company name was taking a beating. And when that happened our own commitment to such people was being called into question, along with our professional integrity, and that was going over the line as far as Tom and I were concerned.

"Jack," Tom whispered, looking off to the side and then back to me. "I know of several partners who made verbal agreements with clients and then conveniently forgot them. Totally unacceptable in my book."

"I couldn't agree more," I said, "though honestly I don't know which is worse, that or what happened with Stan."

Tom leaned back, sipped his espresso, and stared back at me. "That whole thing! Geez. I don't know whether I've ever been that angry in my whole life."

Stan had been one of our marketing people. He seemed fine at first and actually came highly recommended, which in the aftermath of what happened is troubling on a whole other level. Then nearly every month he started making frequent trips out of state, each time for several days. Most of them involved airline flights in business class. He always ate at the finest restaurants. His expense reports grew more extravagant each time. But, hey, he was wooing clients, or so we thought. He'd come back with glowing reports of new business opportunities he'd uncovered. At first we believed him, but then things weren't adding up. He always *talked* about new opportunities when he returned to the office, but we noticed that there was little to no follow-up and scant evidence of once promising leads actually panning out. In the end not a single one of Stan's trips led to any new business. What he had been selling were sheer fantasies, and the only people buying them turned out to be us.

"We need a major overhaul," Tom said.

"*Major*," I agreed.

"Even if it means we have to do something drastic," he added. "But. . . ."

"But where do we begin?" I said, finishing his sentence.

"Exactly."

"It's almost as though we need an entirely new structure to build on," I said, "a new foundation. We need to search our corporate soul and determine what's most important to us."

"Our principles, our convictions, our values," agreed Tom. He put his coffee cup down. "Yes, that's it! We need to take a long, hard, maybe even a harsh look in the mirror. We need to identify our values and clarify which ones we need to be guided by."

Now *I* sat back, arms folded. My body was in Georgia, but my thoughts had drifted back to wintry Chicago, to that ballroom where I labored to listen to one of our self-absorbed and misguided leaders while aware of Jerry's presence.

I smiled. "Tom, I think it's time we came up with our own mission statement."

Tom sighed. "Yeah, but have you ever read some of the typical corporate value statements?"

"Not really," I confessed.

"Well, I've read quite a few over the years. They usually lean more toward political correctness rather than any credible substance. They focus far more on things like protecting the environment and promoting diversity than on outlining internal values that actually guide people within an organization."

"I'm in favor of tackling those other issues as much as anyone, " I said, "but it almost sounds as though those corporate statements are more concerned with public *perception* than public service."

"Exactly."

"So," I said, "what then? How do we put something together that might actually create an ethical and professional structure worth hanging the balance of our future business lives on?"

Again came a deep sigh from Tom. "That," he said, "I do not know."

———

On the way home I couldn't determine whether I felt better or worse than when I first awoke that morning. It was always good to talk things through with Tom, but considering that he sounded just as lost and hopeless as I did, on this particular morning I left him feeling even more confused than before. As I neared our neighborhood, my mind was on Jerry again. I remembered what happened to him in the days following his epiphany and personal mission statement: he was fired. What if Tom and I were headed down a similar path? Were we really prepared to take that chance, to possibly mortgage our futures because we had come to a moral and ethical roadblock fueled by our convictions?

Even on a winter Saturday in Georgia, I began to sweat inside my car. Small beads formed on my forehead. My undershirt became damp.

What were Tom and I thinking? Anyone on the outside would say that we had great jobs. We were well compensated; our families were happy; we had kids at good colleges and others now enjoying the early stages of their own families. Why mess all that up? I was convinced that Tom was going to win his bout with cancer, sign a new lease on life, and then the best days for both of us would lie ahead. Why let our convictions disrupt the path we were on? If we just hung in there for another decade or so, we could spend our days relaxing on a beach, lazily playing eighteen holes, fixing up the mountain house, and watching our grandkids grow older. All we had to do was to suppress the twisting feeling in our stomachs, the unsettling wave of discontent with the way things were, the knowledge that somewhere out there were clients suffering because of our company's compromised principles and practices.

If the driver of the UPS truck hadn't been paying far better attention than I was, it's highly unlikely I would have survived the next moment of my life. Even though I had traveled home this way a thousand times, even though I knew the roads as well as the mailman, somehow I missed the stop sign. The UPS truck was coming from my left and traveling at the posted speed limit, thank goodness. A few miles per hour faster and we undoubtedly would have collided in the middle of the intersection.

He laid on the horn and slammed on his brakes, the screeching penetrating my closed car windows. I hit my brakes too, but only after I was already a few feet beyond the stop sign. My car skidded all the way into the center of the intersection. When I finally came to a stop, the front grill of the truck was inches from my door. I peeled my hands off the steering wheel and looked up. The UPS driver was staring down at me, his face beet red and his breathing clearly labored. He mouthed a few choice words in my direction. I mimed "I am so sorry" in return.

After another moment of staring at each other, he waved his hand violently at me. *Well go on then! Get out of the way!* I took my foot off the brake and slowly, sheepishly, proceeded the rest of the way through the intersection and off to the shoulder. I closed my eyes and tried to steady my breathing.

What was happening to me? Why was my normally steady, collected mind betraying me? This funk I was in had now nearly gotten me killed. *Come on, Jack,* I coached myself. *Pull yourself together.*

I don't think I exceeded five miles an hour the rest of the way home. I parked the car and got out, then walked to the curb to collect the mail before going inside. There was the typical assortment of Saturday ads and promos, a bill or two, the usual credit-card offer, and a personal letter for Katherine. As I walked across the lawn to the front door, still seeing the image of the UPS driver staring down at me, something fell out of the stack of mail and fluttered to the ground. I reached down to retrieve it. It was a travel brochure featuring a tropical island panorama complete with a shimmering seascape, white sand beach, and a couple in much better shape than Katherine and I strolling hand in hand along the shore. The words across the top of the picture caught my eye even more than the picture itself: *Want to get away?*

Did I want to get away? Yeah, more than at any other time in my life. And not back up to Chicago. I wanted that island. I wanted to dip my toes in that ocean. I wanted to clear my head and walk like that with Katherine along a sandy beach. Although I felt a world of uncertainty about the future, I suddenly had no doubt about what I wanted to do in the present.

I pushed open the front door, entered the house, and found Katherine in the study, her eyes transfixed on the computer screen. A wave of guilt rushed over me as I remembered how I had left her that morning, how the door's closing had cut her off in mid-sentence.

"Honey," I said in my most apologetic tone. "I'm so sorry about this morning. I know you were only trying to help me, and I left abruptly. You were saying something as I walked out. Forgive me, but I didn't catch the last thing you said."

She turned away from the computer to look at me. "I was saying," she began, "that I really think we need a vacation."

For the first time all day I smiled.

2

The Island

He was not the only horse watching the daily parade of men rushing about all around him. To his left and to his right were other stalls filled with similarly bridled horses. He could sense the anxiety in every stall. Known to the men and silently understood by the horses was the reality that, while all might be needed, only a few would be chosen.

The Beechcraft seaplane dipped her wing and rolled to the left as I caught my first full view of the island. I knew immediately that this had to be the same angle from which the photographer had shot the brochure spread. It was breathtaking. Somehow Katherine had managed to sleep during the entire flight from Atlanta to Miami, most of the flight from Miami to San Juan, and even dozed off for thirty minutes of our short hop from Puerto Rico to our island. I, on the other hand, hadn't caught a wink. I kept thinking about Tom's words and Jerry's warnings and my own increasingly blurry questions about the future of our business and my own life for that matter.

As the pilot lined up for our landing, I nudged Katherine. "You don't want to miss this, honey," I said gently, tapping her on the shoulder. "It's pretty amazing."

She stirred, sat up, and looked across me out the window. "Wow," she whispered. "Just, well, wow."

After we had landed, a cheery man and two attractive young ladies greeted us as we deplaned. The women wore grass skirts and not so modest coverings, and the man was dressed like a cruise-ship captain. For a moment Katherine and I felt as though we were on a surprise episode of the old show *Fantasy Island*.

"Welcome, welcome!" said the captain. "Welcome to the place of your dreams!"

One of the ladies stuck a flower over Katherine's ear and kissed her on both cheeks. "Welcome, madame," she said, and taking Katherine's hands in hers. "Our hope is that here among the sea and the sand you will find everything you've ever longed for, and lose everything that has ever weighed you down."

Katherine, clearly a little taken aback and perhaps still not fully awake, nodded and said softly, "Well, thank you."

The other grass-skirted greeter draped a necklace around my neck and kissed my cheeks as well. I looked down. At the end of the necklace hung an oyster shell.

"This shell once held a beautiful, priceless pearl," she said. "It represents the hope and the possibility of treasure that you too might find here on the island. We hope you will fill its empty chamber with the essence of a life well lived. But beware: not every shell holds such promise."

That didn't sound so positive to me, not nearly as encouraging as Katherine's greeting. "I don't quite understand," I replied, trying to be kind and forcing a smile.

"What she means," explained the captain, stepping forward, "is that you have the power to change the fortune of your own shell. Your spirit can cause the shell to be filled with blessing or. . . ." He paused, and the idling plane engine behind us drowned out his voice.

"Or what?" I insisted.

"Or your spirit can leave the shell devoid of blessing, without treasure and empty."

We all stood there for a minute in a somewhat awkward silence before Katherine said, "Well, I'm sure Jack's shell is going to be bursting with blessing and promise." Then, her instinctive Southern manners taking over, she added, "And we are delighted to be here on your island."

"As we are equally to have you!" said the captain. "Now let us help you with those bags and show you to your cabin. The richness of the island awaits you!"

———

The accommodations were everything the brochure had indicated. Our bungalow was set off on its own, tucked between a stand of palm trees and a secluded stretch of white beach. It was small and simple, but colorful and breezy and beautifully decorated. The back was all glass, providing a breathtaking view of the ocean. The sliding door was fully open, a nice touch on the resort's part, and we could hear the waves lapping against the shore, accompanied by tropical birds singing in the trees that sheltered the bungalow. A king-size bed, complete with a netted canopy, faced toward the sea. Outside on the porch I could see a Jacuzzi, a covered swing, and, further out, at the end of a wooden walkway a small gazebo where I'm sure many a soul had studied the horizon and wondered about the contents of his or her shell.

An overly happy bellhop in khaki shorts and a flowered shirt helped us with our bags and explained our dining options—there were three restaurants on the island for us to choose from—and then left us alone.

As soon as he was out of earshot, I took off the necklace and plopped it down on the dresser. I turned to Katherine and asked, "So, what in the world was all that business about this ridiculous shell? About my spirit and treasure and blessing?"

"Oh, don't pay that stuff any mind, honey," she said. "I think it's just a part of their shtick, being dramatic and mysterious. I think they're trying to match the drama of the setting, that's all."

"Yeah, maybe," I replied, a bit unconvinced, "but why didn't they say the same thing to you? Where is your shell? It's almost like they know."

"Know what?" Katherine said, reaching her arms up to me and wrapping them around my neck.

I wasn't yet ready for her affection. The captain's words kept ringing in my ears. I gently removed her arms and turned away from her to look toward the sea. I stepped to the open doorway. Katherine came up behind me and began to massage my shoulders. It felt too good to shy away from, and I gave in, rotating my neck to enjoy the full effect of her kneadling fingers.

"Know what, sweetheart?" she said.

"It's almost as though they were looking inside me and reading my brain. Like they know what I'm going through at work, about all my frustrations, about Chicago, about Jerry."

"Jack, come on. Don't you think that maybe *you're* the one who's being a little too dramatic? These people aren't mind-readers. But maybe they. . . . I mean, perhaps. . . ."

I cut her off and turned to face her. "Perhaps what?"

"Well. . . ." She was measuring her words now, I could tell, caught in that place that all spouses are from time to time. She was deciding how honest she should be with the one she loved most and wanted to hurt least. "Well, I imagine these folks are trained in sensing tension and stress. Who knows? Maybe some of them left such lives for the peace and calm of this very place."

I looked in my sweet Katherine's eyes, marveling at how she always remained so calm and intuitive, receptive to things I seemed to miss.

"Regardless," she continued, "they only want to help you, to help *us*. They want this place to do what it's advertised to do—to leave us refreshed and rejuvenated. Never mind the language they use, the particular words, and the psychology behind their thinking. They just want us to leave this place in a better frame of mind than the one we arrived in."

Now *I* reached out to Katherine. I put my arm around her, and we both turned toward the ocean. We stepped out onto the porch together.

"Yeah, I guess you're right," I admitted. "I guess I should be open to anyone who's trying to help me. And, hey, no matter what anyone says, you can't beat this, can you?" I waved my other hand toward the horizon.

"Well," Katherine said, smiling. "We wanted to get away, right? I think you could safely say this is '*away*.'"

"It's absolutely gorgeous, even more so than that glossy brochure."

"You know what else I think?" she said.

"What's that?"

"I think that necklace looked kind of cute on you."

"Cute?" I challenged her. "I'm 54 years old. I'm not looking for cute anymore."

She pressed herself against me and looked into my eyes.

"Let me rephrase that," she said. "Your shell is nothing short of sexy."

I kissed her then and instantly felt some of the tension drain from my body. She kissed me back, and we held each other for a moment. Then we stepped back into the bungalow, and I closed the door.

3

Capsized

As with the other horses, the unknown troubled him. How could it not? He had experienced war before as a young stallion brought along out of necessity, their camp having been razed and burned to nothing. Tied for weeks to makeshift posts, he had pawed at the ground underfoot, brayed and snorted, as the hostilities came closer, moved away, and then returned. All the while he saw the reality of death and desperation yet also the possibility of victory. He took it all in and filed it away. Slowly but purposefully he was preparing himself. His day would come. He wanted to be ready.

The sun had been up for an hour when I awoke the next morning. I rested on my elbows and looked out the wide glass window toward the sea. Katherine was already out on the porch and sitting in the swing, no doubt enjoying the rhythmic therapy of the waves lapping against the shore. Katherine had been a beach girl all her life. She grew up vacationing with her family on the Georgia coast every summer. I instead was a mountain man, having spent many a weekend in my youth alongside my brothers and father roaming the mountains of north Georgia, looking for that perfect camp site and magical trout stream. I wouldn't say that Katherine had converted me, but she certainly had helped me discover the splendor of the oceanside world. Now I too was drawn to its rhythms.

In the kitchen I filled a cup with fresh coffee and went to join her on the porch. "Good morning," I said as I stepped outside.

She turned to look at me. "No, *great* morning," she corrected me.

I smiled and took a sip of coffee.

"How did you sleep?" she asked, a little hesitantly, no doubt wanting so badly for me to escape the funk I was in. I could hear it in her voice and sense it in her spirit.

"I haven't had a night's rest like that in a long time," I said.

"I'm so glad."

I sat beside her on the swing and wrapped my arm around her shoulder. We sat in silence for a few moments, both lost in the scenery before us.

"Well," she broke the silence. "What shall we do today?"

"I propose that we stay like this for as long as we can. Then let's eat some breakfast, followed by a whole lot of nothing."

"I like the sound of that," she replied, tucking her head into my neck.

We ate a late breakfast at one of the resort restaurants down by the beach. The food was fantastic. There were omelets made to order, fresh fruit grown on the island, and an endless supply of breads and pastries baked that morning. And the best part was that neither one of us had to cook or clean up any of it.

Afterwards we went for a long walk along the shore. About a quarter mile down the beach I spotted a rental hut and was drawn to the sight of long kayaks turned over out front.

"You think they rent those?" I said out loud.

"Something tells me that's the idea."

"Yeah, dumb question, I guess."

Holding Katherine's hand, I walked toward the hut.

"Wait a minute," she said. "What happened to doing a whole lot of nothing?"

"Yeah, I know, but I've always wanted to take one of those things out in the ocean. We used to kayak down slow rivers up in the mountains when I was a kid, but that was nothing like this."

"Yeah, nothing like this at all." Katherine sounded worried. "The ocean is no lazy river, Jack. You have to know what you're doing. And look how narrow those boats are. Don't you think you're a little too old for that?"

"I wasn't thinking of going alone," I said, smiling down at her.

"Oh no. " She shook her head. "You're not getting *me* on one of those things. I'm sticking to the original plan—a whole lot of nothing. And I was planning on accomplishing that *with* you."

I pointed to a sign on the front of the rental hut: "*Kayak rentals limited to one hour.*"

"It's only for an hour," I pleaded, giving her my best sad-puppy face.

"Look," she said. "If that's how you want to spend your time, you have my blessing. This trip isn't just about *us*; it's also about *you*, and I want you to get the most out of it. If you think that kayaking out on the sea all day will help. . . ."

"It's an hour, sweetheart, not the entire day. *One hour.*"

She put her arms around my neck and looked hard into my eyes. "Be careful, Jack. Okay? Promise me that?"

I nodded. "Absolutely. I promise."

———

After we returned to the room, changed into beachwear, and packed a day bag, Katherine compromised and accompanied me back to the rental hut. I knew that she was simply worried and wanted to be where she could keep an eye out for me, but I gladly accepted her protectiveness because, in all honesty, I wasn't so sure about this sea-kayaking thing myself. It wouldn't hurt to have someone on the beach who was paying attention to my little adventure.

Why I wanted to do this in the first place wasn't all that clear to me. If I were completely honest with myself, I think I was a bit afraid that if I lay on the beach all day, if I stayed idle, my mind would drift back to places I didn't really want to go—work, Chicago, Jerry McGuire. Taking the boat out seemed like a perfect way to remain blissfully detached from all those things that had been weighing so heavily on me since that ill-fated business seminar. It was with this mindset that I approached the lean-muscled and perfectly tanned manager behind the counter at the rental hut.

"Hello," I said.

"Hallo, mon," he replied in a breezy Caribbean twang. "What can I do ya for t'day?"

I explained that I wanted a kayak for an hour, no more and maybe even less, just to try my hand at it. He nodded, asked my height to determine the correct paddle length, and began to fill out a form.

"Was it dangerous?" I asked. The question was meant partly for Katherine, so that I could give her an answer to ease her anxiety, but also for myself to alleviate my own slightly suppressed concerns.

The manager pointed toward the sea. "Now come on, mon. Look there at the ocean this morning. See how sleepy she is?"

I looked. He was right. The sea appeared as if it were merely a calm lake, her surface unbroken except for the gentle lapping of tiny waves on the white sand beach.

"She's like a bathtub, my friend. Gonna be asleep alll day. No worries. You can tell the old lady that she can go to dreaming on the beach with no care in the world." He nodded toward Katherine and winked.

I smiled back.

He told me the particulars. Life jacket on at all times. Don't go past the floating platform with the yellow flag anchored about a quarter mile offshore. Stay in sight of the beach and rental hut. If I lost my bearings, look for the red flag raised high above the hut. Do everything I could to stay in the boat, and if by chance I capsized it was best not to try to climb back in on open water but rather to drag the boat to shore or use the floating platform to relaunch.

"But that ain't gonna happen, mon," my newfound friend reiterated. "Not with mother ocean so sleepy t'day." Finally, he told me, and this time he tightened his face to make sure that I took this last instruction seriously, *never* fall asleep while out on the water.

I assured him that I had enjoyed a great night's sleep and was about as awake as anyone could be.

"Well, then," he said. "See you in an hour, mon!"

I charged the rental to our room and dragged the boat to the water's edge. After I had lathered up with sunscreen, Katherine came over and kissed me and reminded me once again to be careful. Then she pulled something from her closed hand and reached up toward my neck. It was the oyster necklace.

"What's that for?" I asked.

"Good luck," she said with a smile.

I leaned in and kissed her again.

"That's what I am choosing to believe *for* you," Katherine added, "whether you want to believe it or not."

"You are way too good to me," I said.

I donned the life jacket; the rental manager helped me launch the kayak; then suddenly I was alone in the vast ocean. I paddled toward the yellow-flagged platform, quickly caught up in the overwhelming sensation of being so close to the power and vastness of the sea. I put the paddle down for a moment and leaned back to take in the full glory of my surroundings. Before I knew it, I had fallen fast asleep.

I have no idea how long I slept, but when I awoke it was as if I had left the previous world and entered another altogether. My peaceful, soothing, almost magical kayak ride across a glassy sea had turned into a nightmare.

The ocean had turned into a roiling mass of whitecaps. The sky was dark and full of stormy clouds. I was in the middle of an all-out squall. The seawater was coming over the kayak in droves, and the biggest surprise was the fact that the boat was still upright. I looked in the direction of shore, at least in the direction I *thought* where the shore was supposed to be, and all I could see was endless expanses of water with no land in sight. If there were a red flag out there somewhere, it was nowhere to be seen.

I grabbed the paddle, which miraculously was still in the boat, and began dipping it into the stormy water, trying to steer in *any* direction. After a few minutes I realized that the action was futile. The waves were too high and too strong for my flimsy paddle to gain any traction. I kept trying, though. And I kept getting more and more frustrated, angry, and, finally, downright irate. Whatever peace and relaxation had come over me in the hours since we had arrived on the island seemed as far away now as Atlanta itself.

Then, as if things couldn't get any worse, it started to rain. Hard. I held the paddle up in the air, pointing it toward some unseen force that I imagined must be looking down on me with wrath. "Why me?" I screamed into the eye of the storm. "If anyone is up there, then tell me why this is happening to me. What have I done to deserve this?"

No reply, as if I really believed that were even possible. Just more thunder and the crashing of waves and now, off in the distance, lightning.

"Is anyone out there?" I yelled, "Mother Nature? God? Jerry? Somebody, *anybody*, help me!"

I was completely undone. I might never again see Katherine or my kids or grandkids. A part of me felt like just giving up, but then something happened that rendered even my paddle useless. The end of the blade somehow caught in my oyster necklace. It jerked and pulled my head down. In a panic I brought the paddle down hard against the kayak. It made contact and split in two.

I looked at the two pieces, one in my hand and the other floating away from me. Then, like the proverbial nail in the coffin, a rogue wave hit the kayak broadside, dumping me into the ocean. I reached up and tried to wrap my arms around the hull, knowing that if I were separated from the boat it would surely be the end of me. When I did, I inadvertently rolled the lightweight boat on top of myself. As another strong wave hit the hull, the kayak's middle section slammed directly into my head. Everything went blurry as I felt my hands slip off the hull., The last thing I remembered seeing was the oyster necklace beginning to sink in the water. Then came darkness.

4

Man In the Mirror

It was a reality that he as well as the other horses were forced to accept. Taking a beast into battle that was not ready for combat could mean not only death for rider and animal but also tactical disaster. Ignoring height or mass, those that could not handle the chaos of war would be left behind. It would be their fate to pass their remaining days living under the rule of a victorious enemy.

None wanted to face such a reality, yet not all were ready. It was understood and quietly accepted that some steeds would not see the outside of their stalls again before the matter was settled.

I awoke with the taste of sand and salt heavy on my tongue. My eyes slowly opened, and I discovered the reason: I was lying in the surf on the edge of a beach with my face half-submerged in seawater. I squinted into the full sun and slowly lifted my exhausted body until I was sitting upright. Rubbing sand from my eyes and face, I took a quick inventory of my extremities—everything seemed intact—and then attempted to stand. I immediately became light-headed and sat back down. I sat there for a few minutes scanning my surroundings. About fifty yards down the beach I could see the kayak overturned and half-buried in the sand but seemingly in one piece. There was no sign of the broken paddle, not that a two-piece kayak paddle would do me much good anyway. I looked down at my life jacket, which had no doubt kept me from drowning. I thought of all those times I had neglected to wear one while kayaking in the rivers of north Georgia, and I shuddered now at the possibility of what might have happened had I ignored the rule to keep this one on at all times.

When I sat up a little bit straighter, my hand fell on something in the sand. I looked down. It was the necklace. For a moment I just stared at the oyster shell. I imagined that it was staring back at me, its wide opening like an ever-present eye mocking me. Suddenly, overcome by a surge of unbridled rage, I picked up the necklace, closed my fist around it, stood to my feet, and hurled the shell as far as I could out into the ocean. I studied the water for a minute more, then brushed the sand off my hands and turned to face the beach. That's when I discovered a most unsettling reality.

This was not the beach from which I had launched the kayak. In fact, it looked nothing like the area surrounding the resort. There was no rental hut with a high-flying red flag, no beach chairs with fancy umbrellas. Most notably, of course, there was no sign of Katherine. This beach was also much narrower than that at the resort, and the sand here quickly gave way to thick jungle.

I reasoned that I must have drifted around a point and out of sight before the storm came up. Surmising that my beach must be on the far side of the last line of trees I could see in the distance, I walked in that direction. When I reached the half-submerged kayak, I pulled it out of the water and up onto the beach. Then I flipped it upright and left it to dry. I kept walking until I reached the end of the sandy beach. Then I climbed up onto a rock outcropping that stretched from the edge of the jungle out into the sea. From my high post I could see around the jutting point and far into the distance. To my shock and amazement, not only was my beach nowhere to be seen, but there was no beach at all. Instead dramatic cliffs plunged directly into the ocean as far I could see. There were no signs of life, no signs of civilization. Indeed, it was clear that I was on a wholly different island.

Suddenly I felt overwhelmingly alone.

Jumping down from the rocks, I half-walked, half-jogged the span of the narrow beach and looked in the opposite direction. I discovered the same thing. This island was much larger than the one where we had landed less than twenty-four hours ago, and it was seemingly devoid of human life.

Puzzled and alarmed, I returned to the middle of the beach and sat down on the edge of the kayak. That's when I noticed a path, or at least what appeared to be a path. Upon closer inspection it might only have been an animal track, but it was clear that it led to something *somewhere.*

I peered into the thick brush and studied the dark tunnel cut into the jungle. Then I glanced back along the beach and stared for a long moment out to sea. I silently questioned the wisdom of abandoning this open area where help might reach me, where a plane might pass by overhead or a boat might venture ashore in search of me. Then, sighing deeply, I ducked my head under a branch and disappeared into the forest.

———

Immediately I noticed the absence of light. The sun was still relatively high in the sky, but the cover of thick trees, tangled vines, and branches made for a darkening canopy. I could see only ten or fifteen feet ahead of me. Sometimes the vegetation would get so dense that I had to pry several branches and vines out of my way before continuing, yet the path at my feet remained clearly defined. There was no question that someone, or some *thing*, had forged this path, most likely over a lengthy period of time. The woods were eerily quiet. I heard nothing except my own footsteps and heavy breathing, the latter growing in volume as I pushed on. Now and then I would stop and look back, just to make sure that I could still see the path behind me, in case this might be the only way in or out. I again questioned my decision to enter the woods in the first place. What if the path led to nothing? What if I couldn't find my way back? How long should I continue before giving up?

I then noticed that some light was starting to filter through the canopy. Ahead I could see that the trees were starting to thin out. I pushed my way through the last stand of brush before the jungle cleared and I stood on the edge of a small meadow. At the other end of the clearing was a modest bungalow, oddly eight-sided and seemingly out of place here in the middle of nowhere, yet for a reason I couldn't explain the feeling I had was one of peace, not fear.

The sun was dropping rapidly now, and dusk was beginning to settle around the island. Through a window I could see a light inside the small house. I crossed the meadow and stood at the door of the bungalow. I breathed deeply and knocked. After a few minutes I started to knock again before noticing that the door was slightly open, just enough to betray the light I had seen from the edge of the trees. I pushed the door wide open. The light came from a reading lamp sitting atop an end table positioned beside a large, comfortable-looking reading chair. The rest of the room was bathed in the half-light of dusk.

"Hello," I said. "Is anyone here? I'm lost and need some help."

No response. I waited a moment more and then stepped slowly inside. There was a small kitchen to my left. A teapot rested on the stove, and I could see steam coming from it. Beyond the kitchen was another door leading perhaps to a bedroom. I called toward it, "Hello? My name is Jack. I'm lost, and I just need to use a phone, maybe a two-way radio if that's possible? Don't mean to bother anyone. I just need some help." Still, only silence.

I slowly stepped across the room toward the chair. On a coffee table in front of it was a large leather-bound book opened in the middle. Beside the book was a cup of what looked to be tea, newly brewed, the steam still wafting up. There were fresh stains on one of the pages. It seemed that whoever had been reading had accidentally spilled some of the hot tea on the book.

I leaned over the table, momentarily forgetful of my circumstances and curious about the book. Because of the angle, I had to strain my neck to see what was written on the stained pages.

"Well, hello there." A voice behind me pierced the silence, and I whirled around, ready to explain or defend myself, whatever the moment might demand. In the process I hit the table, and the cup of hot tea spilled completely over.

"Well, guess I'll need more towels," said the voice. "Looks like you've finished what I began."

The voice was that of an old man, at least twenty-five years my senior, maybe more. He wore blue jeans and sneakers with a T-shirt underneath a thin fleece pullover. I was struck by the thought that he dresses a lot like I do when I'm loafing around the house. Apparently he had become chilly in the afternoon storm. That explained the hot tea on a tropical island.

"Don't worry," he said. "You didn't startle me. I heard you when you came in. I was just too preoccupied to answer, looking for a towel to clean up my spill."

"You startled *me*," I said.

He started to walk over to where I stood by the desk. "Let me get that before it soaks in any further."

"Oh," I said, apologetically. "Yeah, I'm really sorry about that."

"Not to worry, son, " he said. In my late fifties it felt odd to be called "son" by anyone other than my own father.

The old man came close, and as he passed our eyes met and I recoiled. My knees grew a little weak, and I had to reach out for the chair to steady myself. Suddenly I realized why he dressed like me.

"You, you . . . ," I stammered, completely undone by what I now saw in his face.

"I know, " he said nonchalantly. "It seems really strange at first."

"You . . . you look just like *me*! Or at least an older version of me," I added.

"Yeah, but there's a good reason for that."

"A good reason?"

"Yes," he said, "because . . . ."
I cut him off. "Because why?"
"Because, Jack, I *am* you."

———·———

Suffice to say, I wasn't exactly sure how to respond to this statement. Was it a joke? A zinger meant to elicit some particular response from me? After he said it, the old man casually went over to the table where he cleaned up the spilled tea before taking the cup over toward the tiny kitchen, presumably to pour another. Over his shoulder he asked, "Would you like something to drink? You can join me for tea. Or I have soda, water, local beer, coffee, as you like."

"Well," I said, "based on what you just told me, I might need something a good bit stronger."

He laughed. "I've got just the thing." I heard a cabinet open and close; then a minute later he reappeared. "The last of a bottle of good Scotch," he said, and handed me the drink. "Now I'll be forced to open a new one soon." He smiled.

"Perfect," I replied, taking a sip.

He returned to the kitchen, finished making his tea, and then came out to join me. "Please," he said, motioning to some chairs, "have a seat."

I hesitated. "Well, um, I'm a bit damp. Fell overboard, you could say. I hate to get your furniture wet."

"My goodness," the old man exclaimed. "How bad a host am I? Let me get you some dry clothes. After all, we're more or less the same size." He winked as he said that last sentence.

He disappeared into the back room and then returned with a set of clean, dry clothes—sweatpants, athletic shorts, a T-shirt, and a pullover. "Those flip-flops by the front door should fit," he said. "You can take them when you leave. I have several other pairs."

He led me to a small bathroom between the kitchen and back room. I changed, carried my wet clothes out to the front porch to dry, and then slipped my feet into the sandals he had indicated. Back inside, I sat in one of the chairs and happily re-engaged my glass of Scotch. I sipped the drink and stared at the old man. I felt as though I were looking into some kind of time-lapse mirror. He looked back at me.

"I know it's kind of strange, " he finally said, breaking the silence.

"*Kind of* strange? That's a huge understatement."

He laughed. "Come on," he said. "Don't you think that's a little overdramatic?"

My response was immediate. "I fell asleep on a placid blue ocean; I awoke in a hurricane; I found myself on a mysterious island; I pushed my way through a dense jungle; and now I'm having drinks with a man who looks like and claims to be me." I paused to take a sip of my drink. "I don't think anything I say or do could get much more dramatic than that."

"I guess you have a point there, " he agreed.

"Well," I said, "do you at least have a name?"

He lowered his eyes.

"Oh," I said, realizing what his stare meant to convey. "Jack. Naturally your name is Jack."

He nodded.

"So," I said, trying to be as calm as possible, "how exactly did I get here?"

"I'm not sure."

"What do you mean, you're not sure?"

"Well, I'm assuming you came by boat. After all, we are on an island," the old man said, without the least bit of sarcasm in his voice.

Now I was the one who lowered his eyes.

"You mean you had nothing to do with the storm and the boat accident and the path leading to this cabin?"

"No, nothing."

"Then how did you know I would be here?"

"Actually I didn't."

"Okay, now this is getting even stranger," I said, putting down my glass.

"You see Jack," the old man replied, "I don't really control my own circumstances or those of others. Instead, I kind of take orders as they are given. As unexciting as it might sound, I just kind of show up. I'm put in certain places and given a certain identity at random moments in history when someone needs something on a level unattainable within the parameters of normal life."

"Someone like me, I assume?"

"Yes, so it seems. But I have nothing to do with the circumstances that brought you here, and I'm sorry if those caused you any harm or heartache."

I shook my arm out and rubbed my forehead. "Other than a sore shoulder and a knot on my head, I guess I'm all in one piece."

"Well then," he said, raising his glass toward mine. "Cheers."

We both sipped our drinks, and for the first time since I fell asleep in the kayak, I felt somewhat relaxed.

"So," I began, anxious to ask the question. "Can you explain to me your appearance? I mean, you know, why you look exactly like . . . me?"

"Oh, that's pretty simple."

"I'm looking forward to hearing *this* explanation."

"Let me ask you something, Jack."

"I'm all ears."

"Whom do you trust the most in life?"

I didn't even have to stop to think before I answered. "My wife," I said. "Katherine. She's the wisest person I know."

"Are you sure that's your answer?"

"Now wait a minute," I said, a bit frustrated. "I realize that you are living in some kind of strange, otherworldly realm, but with all due respect how would you know whether my answer is correct or not?"

The old man put his hand across his heart. "Jack, to be honest I am provided with a great deal of information to which only you and I are privy."

"What do you mean?"

"Whoever sends me, whoever assigns me, does not fill my mind with irrelevant information, but I do benefit from an awareness of all you know about any subject we are discussing at the time."

I pondered this for a moment before speaking. "So, if I understand correctly, you're saying that you know if I give you an answer that is not 100% true?"

"Exactly," the old man said. "Even when you *think* that you are answering correctly."

"And on this point I am not?"

"No," the old man confirmed. "Think a little harder, a little deeper. Whom do you trust more than anyone else on earth? The person you trusted the most even before you met Katherine."

I looked out the window of the cabin. It was completely dark now. Obviously I would not be making it back to my island tonight. I wondered what Katherine must be thinking. I'm sure she was beside herself, worried sick about where I was and feeling helpless to do anything for me. For ME! That must be the answer the old man was trying to pull out of me.

"You mean me?" I said.

"Exactly!" The old man seemed genuinely delighted that I had solved his little riddle of a question. "There is no one on earth you trust more than yourself. The truth is that most people are exactly the same, whether they realize it or not. It's just human nature. Trusting ourselves makes us feel in control, whether we are or not."

Now I understood. "So you're saying that you're appearing to me as me because I'll trust you, or rather myself, more than anyone else?"

"Bravo, Jack, bravo."

I took a moment before asking my next question. A part of me wasn't certain that I wanted the answers it might bring. "And what is it," I began cautiously, "that I need from you? What do you have to tell me that I need to trust?"

The old man smiled. I knew that he was trying to convey something by his smile, but I sensed that it was something I might not be ready for, so I tried to ignore his facial expression.

"You asked me a question about how you got here," said my host, "but let me ask you something, Jack." He leaned back in his chair. "What *brought* you here?"

I played dumb. "I'm not sure what you mean."

"Whoever assigns me doesn't make mistakes," the old man replied. "The one thing I know is that I wouldn't be here to receive you if there weren't a reason for our rendezvous. You must be in search of something."

How could I be sure that this was really happening, that I had stumbled upon some kind of self-reflecting angel in the middle of some hidden rainforest? Could it be that I was merely still asleep in my kayak, drifting lazily off shore with Katherine still in sight? Was I muddled deep in a crazy dream?

"You need some help, huh?" The old man jarred me back to the present.

"Sure," I said, unable to think of a good reason not to accept his assistance.

He crossed his legs and cradled his mug of tea. "This isn't the first time we've met, you know."

"Huh?" I mumbled, caught off guard. "What do you mean exactly?"

"Just that we were together once before. Not so long ago, actually."

"But where? When? I don't claim to have the best memory in the world, but I'm pretty sure I'd recall meeting someone who looked like an aged version of myself."

"No doubt," he countered, "but the first time we met I was sporting a completely different look."

"I'm confused to say the least," I admitted.

"It was cold outside, bitter cold. We were in a room with lots of people. There was a fellow up on a stage talking way too much, in my opinion, and. . . ."

I cut him off. "Chicago? You were in Chicago?" I said, suddenly riveted to his every word. "At our business seminar? But why. . . ?"

Now he cut me off. "I wasn't there by formal invitation. I was there for one reason only: to see you." He said all of this calmly, unshaken by my change in temperament.

I scoured my memory bank. I remembered virtually every moment of that trip to Chicago, but I couldn't for the life of me recall having encountered the old man.

I was sporting a completely different look. I considered his words. "What a minute," I said, suddenly halted in my mental tracks. "*Jerry?* Are you . . . were you . . . Jerry McGuire?"

The old man smiled again. "Bingo."

Now I was the one who slumped back into his chair. It took a few moments for me to gather my thoughts and speak again. "But why?" I said finally. "Why Jerry?"

"I don't know," answered the old man. "I'm not even sure who he is exactly. But the important thing was that *you* knew, and that's why I appeared that way."

"Well, you see, there was this movie and. . . ." I stopped in mid-sentence, realizing for perhaps the first time since that unsettling moment when Tom Cruise's fictitious character first revealed himself above my shoulder that this had nothing to do with Jerry McGuire. "Never mind," I said.

"The point is, Jack," said the old man, "that something was going on, and whether you knew it or not you were calling out for some help, for some answers."

I was caught. The door had been opened, and I had no choice now but to walk through it. I proceeded to tell the old man everything. I told him about the internal conflict that had been steadily rising to the surface for years. I told him about the struggles at work, the moral and ethical dilemmas that I had been wrestling with for so long and couldn't seem to resolve. I bared my professional soul, explaining the crossroads I had reached in my life and career and the battle inside my heart and mind as to what, if anything, I should do going forward. I admitted that there were times when I felt I was willing to just accept the status quo, continue going through the motions, and live with the weight of compromised convictions and principles on my shoulders. At my age, I told him, maybe I was foolish to hang on to what seemed at times like youthful idealism. Maybe I should just float along toward the horizon of retirement and let the next generation make a stand for values and principles and ethical standards. But then, I confessed to the old man, there was that other side of me, the one that believed in holding on to those ideals and convictions. At the core of my being I knew that it was wrong to accept anything less than what was fair and right, just and true. And this part of my make-up I could not shake. Because my soul kept calling me out, I had left Chicago in a panic, hunkered down in that coffee shop with Tom, traveled with Katherine to our tropical island, and eventually found myself in this surreal jungle hideaway talking to a mysterious *Doppelgänger*. I was in a sweat when I finished pouring all this out to the old man. I realized that I had been wringing my hands and staring down at the floor during my confessional narrative, and when I finally looked up I noticed that my host was smiling, almost laughing.

"You think all of this is funny?" I said. "Is my story amusing to you?"

"No, no," he said. "That's not it at all."

"Well, what then?" I wasn't letting him off that easily, not after I had risked so much honesty and self-exposure.

"You give me hope, Jack."

"I give *you* hope?" I said, confused by his comment.

"That's right," he replied, sitting up and almost leaning toward me. "So many men at your age wouldn't even listen to that inner voice that is resounding inside you. Facing the turmoil you've just described, most would do exactly what you said. They would drift into the future, rest on their laurels, level out at some personal and professional plateau. They would let go of the things that propelled them when they were younger, that inspired and drove them to success in the first place."

I looked down again, digesting what he had said and letting out a sigh of emotional exhaustion.

"The fact that you have arrived at this crossroads and decided to consider your next course of direction with such sincerity gives me hope for humanity."

"Well," I said, unsure of how to respond to his affirmation, "I'm glad you didn't waste the last of your Scotch on someone who had nothing to give back."

"So, what's next?" asked the old man. "Do you have any idea of where you go from here?"

I put the glass down and rubbed my chin. "No, I don't. And that's what's wrecking my world right now. It seems . . . well, to use the opposite of your word, it seems *hopeless*."

At this he leaned back and chuckled. "Ha, my friend! Something tells me you don't really believe that."

"No?" I said. "And what makes you so sure?"

"Remember," he said, still smiling, "that I am privileged with insight into your soul that even you might not have."

"Yeah, about that, " I said, a little miffed. "It seems like a really unfair advantage."

"Yes, I guess you could say that," he answered.

"So, then, where is the hope? What direction do I take? If you know any answers, let's cut to the quick. I can finish my drink, leave you to your reading, and head back to Katherine and my vacation."

A wide grin spread across his face. "There *is* hope," he said. "But, as with all things truly worth understanding, *your* answers do not come so easily. You've already put in a lot of work and faced a few daunting challenges, but you still have more to do *if* you want answers and, perhaps most importantly, *if* you refuse to settle for anything less than what your soul is demanding. That, Jack, is your crossroads."

I studied his face and let his words sink in. Could I really trust this man? Or, as he had implied, was it more a question of my being able to trust *myself*, my deepest beliefs and convictions?

Without asking me what I was thinking, he nodded. "Yes, Jack. It's all of those things."

I took a moment more, gathering my fortitude before I took the plunge. "Well then," I said, leaning back again in my chair. "Would it be possible to go ahead and open that new bottle of Scotch?"

While he ambled off to refill my glass, I went to the front door of the cottage and opened it, curious about any change in the weather.

"Make sure you look up," the old man said from the kitchen.

"Why?"

"The break in the trees around the meadow affords a spectacular view of the Caribbean sky on a starry night."

"But how do you know that tonight will be. . . ?" I swallowed my voice when I stepped outside and looked up. The sky was majestic. I had never seen such a sky, or perhaps I had never taken the time to pay enough attention. The storm had moved on and left in its wake a blanket of a thousand sparkling lights. I hoped that Katherine was seeing it also, though I imagined she was beside herself and sick with worry.

When I turned to re-enter the house, I noticed that the short path leading up to the door was lined with flat stones, four on each side, for a total of eight. I closed the door behind me. The old man had placed my refilled glass on the octagonal end table and was situating a tray of cookies beside it.

"I realize that Scotch and cookies are not complements," he apologized, "but they are all I have in the way of a snack right now."

I thanked him, reached for a cookie, and then abruptly stopped myself. The cookies were also eight-sided! The old man had disappeared back into the tiny kitchen, and I became suddenly aware of octagonal shapes *everywhere* including picture frames on the walls, end tables, lampshades, a map of the Caribbean, a set of coasters on the dining table, and a flowerpot in the center. All were octagonal in design, even the throw rug beneath our feet. The scene was suddenly and strangely eerie to me.

When the old man returned to his chair, took a cookie, bit it in half, and realized that I was staring at him, he asked, "What's the matter?"

"All the octagons," I replied, gesturing in a sweeping motion with my hand. "You seem to have some kind of fascination with that particular shape."

He swallowed the rest of his cookie and chuckled. "I was wondering how long it would be before you noticed," he said. "Did you happen to notice the meadow's outline when you first arrived?"

I confessed that I had not but guessed, "Octagonal?"

He nodded. "Yep."

"So, what gives? Why octagons?"

"It's not about the shape. It's about the eights."

"The eights?"

"That's right. The number eight."

"What about it? Number of children? Grandchildren? An old high-school jersey number?"

"Oh no, nothing like that. You see, all of life rests on the number eight."

"Really?" I said, and then added sarcastically, "I've never heard that before. I always thought it was seven or three or some other number more famous than eight."

"Nope. It's eight," he said, ignoring my sarcasm. "All of life rests squarely on eight major pillars, which are foundational for living, loving, and being."

"And for working?" I asked, my professional quandary still uppermost in mind.

"Absolutely. In most ways the business world is no different than the rest of life. People don't check their standards, beliefs, and convictions at the door when they enter an office, even though at times they might pretend to do so. The stones represent principles for *all* of life, a framework for existence or what I like to call 'The Great 8,' a collection of foundational legacy virtues."

"'Legacy virtues'? Why *legacy*?" I asked.

"Because, if put into practice, they not only impact your life in the present but also define an inheritance you leave behind long after you're gone. In a word, they leave a legacy."

I had to admit that I was intrigued. As a businessman always in search of formulas or systems that could help my company achieve more effective results, I tried to keep my mind open to new ideas and ways of thinking.

Of course, more than not I was disappointed with the latest craze or fad in the corporate world, misled by some *faux* leader type whose inflated ego was light years ahead of his actual ability to produce concrete outcomes. Chicago was only the latest such case, and almost like a last straw for me. Was it really possible that this old man living in the hidden jungle of some mysterious island possessed a deep well of knowledge capable of righting my personal and professional ship? Could all of life rest on his as yet un-disclosed eight principles, or *legacy virtues* as he called them?

"I may not be as old and wise as you," I said, "but if life has taught me anything it's that merely existing, let alone things like relationships and fam-ily and chosen profession, are far too complicated to be captured so simplis-tically. The idea that everything rests on eight essential values, is. . . ."

He cut me off. "*Virtues*, not values. 'The concept of values implies a relative or temporary context, but virtues imply an absolute or permanent context. They have stood the test of time. They can be applied to any era, any culture. 'The Great 8' have universal application."

Suddenly my mind drifted back to my coffee-shop conversation with Tom and our talk about rethinking our corporate and professional values. "Okay," I submitted. "*Virtues*? It still strikes me as far too narrow to believe that all of the world's problems, and all that opposes contemporary busi-ness ethics, can be summed up by eight so-called 'Legacy Virtues.'"

"Fair enough," the old man said as he stood up. "Can I ask you to com-plete a small assignment for me?"

"An assignment?"

"Yes," he replied, moving toward a table. There was another notepad nearby, which he picked up and walked back over to where I sat. "Here's what I want you to do," he said, handing me the pad and pencil. "I've got to clean up some things in the kitchen and put a few things away for the night. While I'm doing that, I want you to think of the most obvious eight problematic issues that plague the business world today. Social ills, you might call them. Vices. I think you will find that they afflict all of life, but for your purposes, if you want to restrict your thinking only to the business world, that will do for now."

I took the pad and pencil with some hesitation. A part of me felt as though this was a silly exercise. Another part of me, however, wanted the challenge, as if this were an obstacle between myself and a successful business venture. The competitive side of my make-up wanted to stump the old man. I wanted to let him know that I possessed a far more sophisticated business acumen than he realized.

"Okay," I said. "Challenge accepted. I just need a few minutes."

"Only a few minutes?" he retorted. "That easy an assignment, huh?"

I looked up. "Unfortunately, I've been in business long enough to see the dark and disappointing side of that arena. I wish that wasn't so, really I do, but you can't spend as much time as I have inside the corporate world without witnessing its shady characters and shadowy corners."

"Well, then," the old man said, heading for the small kitchen. "I guess I'd better take care of my domestic chores in a timely fashion. Apparently I have a star student here."

I watched him disappear into the kitchen, took a sip of my Scotch, and then lifted the pencil.

———

Once the old man had left the room, the blank paper staring up at me suddenly appeared intimidating. For all the times I had witnessed the unethical side of the business world, my mind momentarily went blank. Challenged to list eight discrete business vices, as the old man had labeled them, I was temporarily stymied. Then I thought back to Chicago and similar corporate training events. I also recalled many frustrating conversations with Tom that left us both discouraged, including our last one in Starbucks that indirectly led me to the island and now to the old man's cottage. Soon all my years of experience with the dark and at times unethical side of corporate life came into focus. Over the course of the next few minutes I managed to scribble down literally dozens of social ills that I had seen manifested at one time or another in the business world. I sat back up, looked over my list, and then began scratching out the lesser of these evils until I had pared them down to an even twelve.

"How's it going in there?" the old man called over the sound of running water and clattering dishes. "Harder than you thought, huh?"

"*Please*, " I responded sarcastically. "This is a piece of cake." But as I said it, I felt a droplet of sweat on my brow. The truth is that I was discovering how things were much worse than I had previously thought. For a moment I wondered how I had ever survived so long in the professional arena I had chosen. I leaned in closer to the paper and let my eyes skip from one entry to another, trying to eliminate a few more.

Then, at last, I put down the pencil. I had my eight.

As if he could sense the completion of my task, the old man reappeared, drying his hands on a towel. "Done?" he asked.

"Done," I said, trying to hide my emotional exhaustion.

"How about a glass of water?" he replied, and I could tell that he sensed the tension through which I had labored.

"Sure," I said, the pleasure of the Scotch being a memory now and my mouth parched.

He went back into the kitchen and returned a moment later with a tall glass of water, which he handed it to me before sitting back down in his chair.

"So," he began, "are you ready?"

"You make this sound so serious," I said, "as though you're going to tell me something that will change my life."

He leaned back and spread his hands in front of him. "Why expect anything less?" he asked with a gleam in his eyes. "After all, you traveled a long way to get here, and I don't mean just physically."

"Okay, then," I agreed, though still skeptical. "Teach me, oh wise older version of myself."

I had written my eight words down in no particular order, so I simply read the first one on the page that had survived my cuts. "Egotism."

The old man smiled. "Ah yes, ego, that old internal fire that gives a man the confidence to walk out the door each morning."

"That's just it," I said. "It's really hard to draw the line in life and in business between confidence and ego."

"True enough, but there is a secret that lies between those two, and it makes all the difference in the world."

"Tell me," I said eagerly, this puzzling issue of balance having been one I had tried to comprehend ever since my first years at university. Still ringing in my ears were the words of one academic counselor after another championing pride in one's accomplishments as a way to separate oneself from those willing to accept mediocrity in the classroom or in life.

"*The treasure of the unassuming is possession, in the end, of that which is of highest value.*"

"Huh?" I replied. "You lost me."

The old man laughed and then continued. "If you are too rich in personal perception, then you have little need of anything or anybody. Of course, ego itself is not all bad. It's good to have a positive self-image, to possess a wealth of confidence, but beware: egotism often leads to isolation because it encourages one to think, 'I have all the gifts. I do not need anyone else.'"

As he said this, several people I had worked with other the years came to mind. At first they were the kind of business minds that I deeply admired, was even jealous of, yet slowly, as I came to know them better, I realized they were so egocentric that they were incapable of appreciating or affirming anyone else. Their comments tended to be critical and make others, including myself, feel inferior. I had even known colleagues who would go so far as to lay claim to someone else's accomplishment or, if not directly, credit themselves by saying something to the effect of, "After all, I taught him everything he knows."

"In the short run, " the old man added, "this mindset can actually seem to work in favor of the egotistical person because it creates an environment of dependency and control. People who are averse to risk tend to accept remaining under the authority of an egotistical boss for a long time, but those people are not positive and do not really enjoy their work. They *go along to get along*, but it leads to a very negative culture. Eventually people working alongside or underneath them will come to their senses and say, 'Enough is enough!' Then one day our ego-driven character wakes up to find himself all alone and abandoned, possibly even losing those he tried to rule to a competitor. It doesn't really matter whether we are talking about the business world or life in general. This pattern inevitably repeats itself when someone in a position of authority lets his or her ego trump those he has been appointed to lead."

"So what's the answer?" I said, anxious to hear how the old man reconciled the trap of ego with the healthy platform of self-confidence.

"Legacy Virtue number one." When he paused and looked at me, I realized that he wanted me to write down his next words.

"Yes," I said, now leaning forward.

"*Humility.*"

I leaned back, my body language unable to hide my disappointment. "Humility? But doesn't that indicate . . . well, weakness?"

"Oh no, anything but," the old man countered. "That's an old myth probably begun by one of those egocentric characters we were just referencing. The truth is that demonstrating humility can be an incredibly effective tool for galvanizing people around a common purpose, mission, or cause, a goal if you will, and then leading them toward realizing that goal."

"How so?" I said, not convinced. I had seen too many co-workers fall by the wayside over the years because of what I perceived to be psychological weakness.

"Don't confuse a lack of drive or self-confidence with the ability to humble oneself and rise above, not sink below, the trap of ego run amok."

I scratched my head, trying to absorb all that he was saying.

"In truth, " the old man elaborated, "it takes a certain level of self-confidence and security to be vulnerable enough to express appreciation for others' gifts and talents. A person of humility readily gives credit to

someone who has done good work. This, of course, tends to lead to recip-
rocal affirmation of others within the group. People are much more willing
to follow the leadership of someone who demonstrates humility."

"I guess I never thought about that." As the words left my mouth, the
image of our keynote speaker in Chicago flooded my memory. I recalled
how not too far into his presentation it became clear that he was more
interested in painting himself as a superstar than in inspiring and motivating his audience. The more he spoke about his self-perceived business prowess, the more my colleagues and I started to feel that his main
purpose was to create a separation between himself and us. Perhaps the
worst was all that "A team" nonsense and the implication that we in the
audience were inferior to him. His inflated ego was in fact achieving his
apparent objective. By the end of his monologue, none of us wanted to
be around him!

My mind returned to the concept proposed by the old man.
"Vulnerability and service as a way of cultivating loyalty," I said, pondering
the concept. "Actually it makes a lot of sense."

"And not just loyalty, " the old man went on. "Serving from a humble,
unassuming posture builds teamwork. It brings about a blending of individual gifts and abilities. Humility enables people to forget about themselves long enough so that they can be genuinely interested in the other
people within an organization."

"It makes me think of Aristotle's simple yet profound statement."

"Ah yes, it fits perfectly here."

"'*The whole is greater than the sum of its parts*,'" I quoted.

"Indeed. And when you value the people around you, the virtue of humility counteracts the negative effect of ego."

I scribbled some notes while the old man continued.

"Demonstrating humility from a position of strength means that you
can step back and acknowledge your own shortcomings. After all, none of
us, no matter how learned or experienced, is perfect. At some level all of
us need others. And if we do not invite others to invest in us, to help us
push to the next level in life or in business, we become poor. So I think that

we should actually celebrate our need for others, especially those we are charged with leading, and welcome their input."

"Do you by any chance have an example," I asked, "someone you've come across who epitomizes what you are saying?"

"Oh yes," he answered emphatically. "I have many, but one in particular comes quickly to mind."

"Who?"

"I encountered a man many years ago," he said, lowering his eyes. "Actually several thousand years ago, if you want to know the truth."

Momentarily jolted back into the surreal reality that the man before me was otherworldly, I could only smile at what for him sounded like a rather ordinary event.

"I was sent to help him finish a mission," the old man continued. "He was charged with leading a group of people across a great desolate land. The crossing took decades. There were lots of heartache and suffering along the way. They were a stubborn group, resistant, rebellious, always challenging his authority. He easily could have given up on them, walked away from the mission, and created a much better, certainly easier, life for himself. The people complained, insulted him, again and again telling him that they knew a better way to accomplish their goal. He would patiently listen to them with compassion and, most of all, with great humility."

I listened, fascinated. The old man paused. I could tell that his mind was drifting back across time in a contemplative way. I detected the slightest smile on his lips. "Well," I said, anxious to hear the end result, "what happened?"

"They never stopped questioning his leadership, but his humble approach somehow kept them on course, kept them alive and protected. Eventually, in his twilight years of leadership, he passed the torch on to an understudy, and the mission was completed."

We were both silent for a few moments, the old man reflecting on events in an era long gone, I on many of the things that had troubled me during the last few years at work. And for the first time in a long, long while, I felt something that had been absent in my professional life—hope.

We broke our reverie at about the same time and looked at one another.

"I imagine that today feels like one of the longer days in recent memory for you," he said.

"That might be your *second* greatest understatement," I replied with a laugh.

"Why don't you go on back to Katherine?"

My laugh ended abruptly. "Are you playing games with my emotions?"

"No," he protested, holding up his hand. "I'm completely serious. It's late. We're both tired. Go on back to your island and, if you'd like, come back to see me tomorrow, and we'll continue with your list. We have seven vices and virtues left to cover."

I wasn't sure whether to smile, cry, laugh, or throw something at him. "But how?" I said. "It's dark. My paddle is in pieces. My kayak is probably useless. I would have no idea in which direction to go, let alone the ability to see where I'm going. Besides, I doubt that I could even find my way back to the beach."

"Jack?"

"Yes?"

"We've only known each other a short while, but do you trust me?"

I considered his question. I knew what I wanted to answer. I wanted to shout "No!" I wanted to point out how crazy this whole situation was, how surreal it had become. Yet, for reasons I could not explain, I *did* trust him. I trusted him as if, well, as if he were my own father.

I nodded in the old man's direction. "Actually, I'm not sure why, but, yes, I think I do."

"Okay, good. Now just do what I tell you, and you'll be back with Katherine before you know it."

"I'm listening."

"Go back exactly the way you came, through the woods."

"But it's pitch black outside and I. . . ."

He stopped me. "Jack, you have to trust me on this. Completely. I know that won't be easy, but it's the only way for you to get back to Katherine."

I let out a deep sigh. "Okay," I managed to say.

"When you leave the house, reverse the path you took to get here. Just keep your eyes, ears, and mind open, and you will know the way. Don't worry about the darkness. It won't keep you from finding the beach. When you get there, you will know what to do, I promise."

"And if I want to come back, how do I do that?"

"Ha!" the old man laughed. "Now that part you are not going to like at all."

"It can't be any worse than how I arrived here today."

"No, that's true," he said, still smiling. "Actually that's the *only* way here."

"What?" I said, hoping for a different answer. "I have to go through all of that again?"

"No, it doesn't have to happen *exactly* the same way," he said.

"I'm confused."

"I know this will sound crazy, but when you find yourself out on the sea tomorrow, should you choose to return, don't fight the storm."

"But a storm like that could easily have killed me."

"Could have," he said, "but didn't. And won't."

I studied his face. It was clear that he was completely serious about all of this.

"So, if all of this happens as you say it will, I'll be back on my island, sleeping in the same bed with Katherine tonight, and then I can turn around and be back here again with you in this same place tomorrow?"

He nodded.

"And what do I tell Katherine?"

"That's for you to decide. Maybe everything, maybe nothing. Again, I think you will know what to do. Trust me with the physical journey, but trust yourself with the personal one."

I sat for a minute more and then, not wanting to lose another moment away from my wife, I stood and moved toward the door. The old man remained in his chair.

"Do you want me to lock it as I go out?" I said, reaching for the door handle.

"Ha! When you leave, the population of this island will be down to one. There's no need to lock any doors, and I don't think I'll have any more visitors today. But I hope I have one tomorrow. I enjoyed your company, Jack."

"Well, I'm leaving the notepad here, " I said, gesturing back toward the table.

"I noticed that," the old man said with a smile.

"Okay then. Hope I see you again tomorrow or . . . well . . . whenever."

We exchanged knowing glances. Then I stepped outside and gently closed the door behind me. As expected, the night was inky dark. At first I couldn't see a thing, and then slowly I was able to make out the opening at the far end of the clearing that marked the path. It crossed my mind that maybe the old man had a flashlight I could borrow. I turned to open the door and ask him, but as I did I glanced through the window and saw him slumped down in his chair asleep.

After a deep breath I crossed the meadow, now noticing the octagonal outline the trees made at the perimeter, and stood at the edge of the path. How I was going to see my way to walk more than a few feet I had no idea, but I had determined to take the old man at his word and so, with one last deep breath and summoning my courage, I stepped into the woods.

5

Back to Katherine

One day it happened. The stallion had feared it all along. A storm broke in the dead of night. The wind bashed against the crude frame above the stalls, and the rain gusted sideways. He moved to the deepest corner and turned his head away from the piercing downpour, as if he could keep the sensation at bay. But it came anyway.

Doubt.

Was he good enough? Was he strong enough? Would he be ready if and when they came calling? Could he fulfill the only purpose for which he had been kept? When the critical moment came, when the enemy pressed its advantage, could he live up to the label he so wanted to claim—warhorse.

Almost immediately the moon showed itself high above, and the trees around me seemed to thin, letting in the fullness of night's ultimate beacon. A white glow illuminated the path in front of me. I picked my way through the forest and arrived at the beach. The trek seemed amazingly short. Even more stunning was what I discovered once at my destination. My kayak, looking unblemished and new, leaned on its side against a palm tree at the path's entrance. My paddle, now somehow miraculously back together in one piece, stood against the bow, the life jacket slung around its blade. Instinctively, I looked up and down the beach to see who might have been responsible for this uncanny restoration, but the beach was as desolate and devoid of human life as it had been when I washed ashore earlier on this endless day. Save for the sound of the waves gently lapping at the shore's edge, I was alone.

So far things were unfolding just as the old man had assured me they would. I had found the beach and presumably my transportation back to Katherine. Now all I had to do was to trust his words and find the courage to launch my kayak out into the ocean. This step did not come easily. It was one thing to push my way through a forest in the dead of night, my feet safely on solid ground. But it was quite another to climb into a small boat and push out into a dark ocean with no GPS, no lights in the distance, and unsure of how far or in what direction I would be navigating.

After stalling for a few minutes, hoping for a better option, I let out another deep sigh and then went about the task of dragging the kayak down to the water's edge. I put on the life jacket, grabbed the paddle, and prepared to ease the boat into the shallows. That's when something wrapped itself around the center of the paddle near my hand. It was the oyster-shell necklace. But how could that be? I last saw it sinking into the water just before I lost consciousness. I had assumed that it sank to the bottom of the ocean, thankfully never to be seen again, but now here it was again, returned to haunt me or, perhaps, to *guide* me. I did the only thing that seemed right at the moment. I unwound it from the paddle and replaced it around my neck, where Katherine had fashioned it that morning. Then, without pausing to second-guess myself, I eased the boat into deeper water and slipped inside the cockpit.

I quickly worked my way past the low breakers and out into the open ocean. I paddled for a few minutes and then, remembering that I had no idea which way to chart my course, I lay the paddle across my lap and recalled the old man's words of admonition: "Don't worry about the darkness. . . . [Y]ou will know what to do, I promise."

The stars had returned, and I leaned my head back to marvel at them. I thought about all those nights back home in Georgia when I had ignored them, preoccupied as I was then with mundane matters I found myself feeling a tinge of guilt for myself and the rest of humanity when we fail to appreciate the incredible face of nature that surrounds us.

I studied the stars and thought about my conversation with the old man. I wondered how I would explain everything to Katherine. I wondered whether I should even try. My small boat rose and fell as the sea undulated beneath me. The motion began to calm any sense of fear I might have had about being out on the water at night. I fingered the shell necklace and remembered the words of the woman who greeted us when we first arrived on the island. She had said the shell represented "the hope and the possibility of treasure." At the time I had assumed that she meant some kind of financial fortune, but maybe that was too simplistic. Might she have been alluding to something less tangible, something more ethereal?

I pondered these thoughts and gazed at the night sky. I let the ocean's gentle rhythm soothe my tired body. The stars began to merge, my eyelids began to drop, and before I knew it once again the ocean had rocked me fast asleep.

————

I felt the sunburn before I opened my eyes. I could tell that it was a bad burn and was going to require some serious lotion. When my squinting eyes slowly opened, the first thing I noticed was a white stripe across my stomach where the life jacket had parted. The pain of the sunburn temporarily caused me to overlook the shock of finding myself back in my swim trunks, the clothes the old man had loaned me nowhere in sight. But there was no time to dwell on the mystery. Instead, I sat up abruptly, stunned to see the position of the sun. It was high in the sky, just off center, indicating that the time was somewhere close to noon. Had I really slept all through the night and the following morning and awakened only after the sun had reached its daily summit? Then I noticed something else startling—the floating platform with the yellow flag, the one the rental manager had told me not to venture past. I was in fact beyond it, but only by twenty yards or so.

Reorienting myself based on memory, I turned my eyes in the direction of the beach and immediately spotted the red flag raised high atop the rental hut. I could only hope that somewhere on that beach was my sweet Katherine. I imagined her running up and down the shore, frantically searching the horizon, beside herself with worry and fear but refusing to give up on my return. I had been gone at least twenty-four hours.

By now, I was sure, she had mobilized whatever emergency search personnel were available on the island, perhaps in helicopters or boats. I thus was a bit surprised that mine was the only vessel out on the water and that I didn't notice any signs of activity or urgency near the shoreline. I paddled quickly through the surf, making landfall in a matter of minutes. Yanking the kayak onto the sand, I dropped my paddle and began searching for Katherine.

With so few people on the private beach, I quickly realized that she was not one of them. I looked in the direction of the bar, the outdoor restaurant where we had enjoyed our breakfast, and then over to the kayak-rental hut. There she was! Katherine was talking to the manager, no doubt planning what the next step in the search would be. I walked hurriedly toward the hut. As I approached, it struck me as odd that Katherine was wearing the exact same outfit as yesterday. I don't know how many bathing suits she had packed, but it wasn't like her to wear the same one every day of a vacation. Then I realized, of course, that she had never changed. In her panic and distress she had merely fallen asleep in her bathing suit, likely for only a handful of hours, then resumed her panicked search the following day without a thought of going to the trouble of changing clothes. Then something caught my attention and really puzzled me. The two of them were having a drink. If I didn't know better, it appeared that they were actually laughing, sharing a light moment and perfectly at ease.

"Katherine?" I said, as I reached the rental hut. Maybe my eyes had betrayed me and it wasn't her at all. That would explain the casual demeanor. When she turned, however, I recognized my wife, and suddenly I was overcome with joy and gratitude. Over the last day I had entertained the thought that I might never see her again. I rushed to her now and held her hard against me.

"Jack," she said, clearly flustered at my affection. She stayed buried in my hug for a moment, then politely eased back out of it. "Honey, I'm glad you're back, but this is a little bit embarrassing, you know. The rental was only supposed to be for an hour. You're really late."

Late? I thought. That seemed like an odd way to describe the circumstances. I was a bit stunned and caught off guard.

"Yeah, mon," the rental manager began. "Ya know we have other people here wantin' to go out on the water. Sorry, mon, but I'm gonna have to charge you a late fee." He reached for his clipboard.

"Of course, of course, " I said. "Whatever you need to do. I'm so sorry. I fell asleep and then. . . ."

"Thirty minutes late, Jack," interrupted Katherine. "That's just not like you. Are you okay?"

"Katherine," I said, staring into her eyes. "I'm not sure what you mean. I must have been gone at least twenty-four hours. I fell asleep shortly after I left, and then when the storm hit. . . ."

Now the rental manager interrupted me. "Whatcha talkin' bout, mon? What storm? Look at that sky. It's the same as when you left, my friend. And the ocean, she slept the whole time you were out. She even put you to sleep. I told you to be careful about that, mon. You're lucky. Someone up there is a smilin' on you. Sleeping on the sea can be very dangerous, my friend." He made some notes on his clipboard.

I turned again to Katherine. "Sweetheart, I don't know what he's talking about. I awoke to a storm. I was fighting heavy wind and waves. I lost my paddle. I was worried I might never see you again. I was afraid for my life."

The rental manager mumbled something about a paddle replacement fee. Then the tone of Katherine's voice shifted.

"Jack, I was *watching* you," she said, her words measured and matter-of-fact. "When it was almost an hour, I tried to call out to you, but you were asleep. A while later I finally came over here, and this nice man was about to come out and get you."

I stared back at her incredulously. "But Katherine, that just can't be." My eyes pleaded with her to understand.

She stared back at me. Now she looked more worried. I could tell that she was trying to understand me, to make sense of what I was saying. She looked over at the manager, who was staring back at her and looking confused himself. Then he turned back to me.

"Let me ask you a question, mon. Please forgive me if I'm puttin' my nose where it don't belong, but did you maybe have a few drinks before taking out one of my boats? We have very clear rules about. . . ."

"No!" I half yelled. "I wasn't drinking. It wasn't even noon yet. Listen, I'm telling you. There was a storm. The boat actually capsized." I noticed him looking over to where the kayak lay on the beach.

"She sure looks fine from here, mon."

I turned back to Katherine. "You believe me, don't you?"

She hesitated. "Jack, let's go back to the cottage. It's time for lunch anyway. You are really sunburned. Maybe the direct sun clouded your memory. You probably just fell asleep and had a dream and lost track of time. It's fine. Look, it's really no big deal. It was an accident."

I fell silent.

Katherine put her arm around me and led me away from the rental hut. She apologized to the manager, thanking him for his patience. Then the two of us gathered her things from where they lay on the beach and started walking back to our cottage.

I don't know whether the heat had clouded my memory or not, but I suddenly had an awful headache, and the sunburn was bothering me so that it hurt to talk. I decided I would wait until we were back at the cottage, maybe after a shower and a cold drink, before trying to explain myself to Katherine again. However, I had one final thing I had to ask her right away.

"Katherine?"

"Yes, honey," she said, sliding her arm in mine as we walked.

"You said you were watching me while I was out on the water."

"Yes."

"Did you maybe fall asleep for a while yourself? Was there a period of time when you lost track of where I was? Of the time, maybe? Is that possible?"

"No, Jack. Every few minutes I would look out and find you on the water. I never fell asleep. I was reading. And you were always there."

I didn't say another word the entire way back to our cottage.

———

I took a long hot shower while Katherine set out a lunch brought by room service. She had ordered my favorite, Lobster Reuben sandwiches, no doubt looking for a way to pull me out of my funk.

After my shower she rubbed about a gallon of lotion on my back and shoulders and chest to ease the sunburn. Then we ate on the back patio, looking out at the sea that now seemed like a great mystery to me. We ate mostly in silence, neither of us quite sure how to ease into conversation about the earlier events of the day. I had begun to entertain the possibility that I may in fact have imagined, or rather dreamed, the storm, the hidden island, and the old man. I had to consider that as an option. There was no reason for Katherine to tell me anything other than the truth, and if she had kept an eye on me throughout my kayak ride, how could any of the things I wanted to recount for her be accurate?

"How do you feel?" she asked, breaking the silence. "Better?"

I knew Katherine's voice and inflections well enough to discern that she was still of the mindset that I had only imagined the storm and the kayak's capsizing and my being away so long. She didn't want to say this directly. She was trying to sympathize and listen and play the role of the patient, understanding soul-mate. But I could sense what she was really thinking: that in my recent state of stress I had simply fallen asleep out on the soothing ocean and had a fanciful dream that seemed real. I thought about what Katherine must be thinking and quietly admitted to myself that if I were in her shoes I would have come to the exact same conclusion. And it was in that moment, looking deep into her eyes, that I made the decision not to tell her about the hidden island and the old man.

A part of me instantly felt guilty. After all, Katherine and I shared virtually everything. She was my best friend, my sounding board, my . . . well, my balance. But for some reason, perhaps protecting both of us, suddenly I felt that it would be best not to divulge all the details of what I *thought* I had experienced over the past twenty-four hours. Maybe I decided to keep this to myself because even I still wasn't sure that it really had happened. Whatever the reasons, I decided then and there to keep everything to myself at least for now. I also made a clear determination in that moment that I had to return to the secluded cottage and the old man. I had to know whether it and he were real or whether I had only imagined it all.

"Honey," said Katherine, "do you want to talk about it?" She was employing her kindest, gentlest tone.

"No, it's okay," I said. "Whatever happened today, I'm just glad I'm here with you now. Let's enjoy the rest of the day together. Get back to doing 'a whole lot of nothing.'"

Katherine smiled. "Now you're speaking my language."

And that's exactly what we did, spending the rest of the afternoon on our own patio. We both took catnaps. Katherine read, and I finished a novel I'd begun months before but put aside for lack of time. I even read an article in a business journal, and for the first time in weeks I was able to do so without getting twisted up inside over my frustrations with work.

The article was mostly about a tycoon who had climbed the ladder of corporate America, moving from company to company and supposedly leaving them in better shape, at least fiscally, than when he first arrived. Toward the end of the article the interviewer asked him some lighter questions about family life, hobbies, and friends. The magnate dismissed that side of his life, remarking "Who has time for friends?" He went on to say that it wasn't his goal in life to make more friends but rather to reach his own "maximum personal potential." Said the tycoon, "If doing so attracts others into my inner circle, then so be it. But if not, then the best thing for other people is to let me do my job, get on board or get out of the way."

And what about family? the interviewer pressed. "Oh, they're part of my team," the businessman answered. "They want me to reach my maximum potential as well. If I settled for anything less, I would be causing them to settle too. And let's face it: if I'm happy, then they're happy."

I wondered what his wife would say. If she were free to answer with complete honesty, would she echo his sentiments? What about the man's kids? Then I wondered about myself. Katherine had always been my biggest supporter, but there were times in years past when I know I made choices that were no doubt driven by a desire to achieve professional milestones, regardless of what my family might have thought or wanted. I simply chose not to ask their opinion. I had felt guilty about this even at the time but had suppressed those feelings in the name of what I perceived to be personal and professional advancement. Now, in light of my conversation with the old man, I questioned whether I had simply chosen to listen to my ego instead of considering what was best for those around me, especially those I loved.

I was in no position to judge, but the article made it pretty clear that this businessman possessed one massive ego. I couldn't help but wonder whether a lack of humility had caused those around him to fall away and keep their distance. Maybe his climb "up" was more about *their* letting him go, freeing themselves of the burden of dealing with a myopic, self-driven, and domineering personality at the office each day. What would the tycoon say about the virtue of humility?

Later that night, as I lay awake and listened to Katherine breathing beside me, these reflections flooded my mind. We went to bed with the sliding back door open. Only a thin screen separated our room from the outside, and I could hear the waves rolling in off the ocean and collapsing against the shore. I wondered what lay out beyond those waves. I also speculated on whether the secret island really existed and, if so, whether the old man who looked just like me was somewhere in the middle of that thick jungle sleeping peacefully in his eight-sided bungalow. Soon my mind surrendered to my body, and I drifted off into unconsciousness.

6

Back to the Island

The great horse heard the soldier's voice before he saw him. It was early, the threshold of dawn. His flanks twitched, and he lifted his head, turning it slightly to make out the silhouette of the soldier as he approached. He knew that everything about how he responded at this moment, on this one morning, would determine whether he was chosen or left behind. He breathed nervously through his flared nostrils. I must show strength, he thought, which is something different from power.

At the rail the soldier spoke to him in a way meant to convey his status as master. Even before opening the stall, the soldier was asking him for something and requesting the same in return. The words were offered as a mutual agreement. For what lay ahead, should he be selected, both rider and horse must give to the other that most precious commodity—trust.

Before I asked the question, I knew that Katherine would think I was crazy. We had just finished breakfast and were sitting together on the patio drinking the rest of our morning coffee. Katherine was reading a book, and I was studying the watery horizon. I waited until I sensed it was the right moment, and then I sprang it on her.

"So," I began, cautiously offhand in my delivery, "what would you think if I said that I wanted to rent the kayak again today?"

Silence. Then she lowered her book, and her gaze joined mine out in the distance. "Well," she answered, "you *are* a grown man. I mean, at least physically." She looked over at me and smiled.

"You're funny," I replied, pleased that the exchange was proving to be light.

"And you've always had a knack for learning from your mistakes. I don't really like the idea of us having to pay any more late fees. Do you think you can make it an hour without falling asleep?"

"I've already thought about that," I said. "I think I'll put in for a two-hour rental today, just in case."

After a few more moments of silence she said, "Jack, as I said yesterday, this vacation is for both of us. If that's how you want to spend a few hours of your day, I don't want to keep you from that. Just, well. . . ."

I cut her off, knowing exactly where she was going. "Just be careful," I said. "I know."

"And please put on plenty of sunscreen. If that sunburn gets any worse, you won't want to leave the cottage, and your vacation will be ruined."

"Of course," I agreed. "That's a promise."

Katherine nodded in my direction and then went back to reading.

"Katherine?" I interrupted again.

"Yes?" she said with great patience. Katherine didn't just read books; she immersed herself in them; and I knew that I was hindering her favorite morning ritual.

"Well," I began. "I was thinking I might go out this morning. You know, less sun and all."

Again she lowered her book and studied the horizon. "You know you're really pushing me Jack Harper?"

"Yeah," I confessed. "I know."

"If I didn't love you to death. . . ."

"But you do," I said with a wink.

She sighed. "I cannot tell a lie."

I stood up and moved over behind her and massaged her shoulders for a moment. "You are really amazing," I said. "You know that?"

"Something tells me that you would say anything right now to get your way."

I laughed lightly. "And you know me far too well."

———

Within fifteen minutes we had changed into beach clothes, packed a day bag, and walked halfway back to the main beach where I had rented the kayak the day before. I was a few steps in front of Katherine, my feet moving a bit more briskly than hers.

"Slow down, cowboy," she admonished me. "The ocean isn't going anywhere, you know."

I tried to heed her request, but my legs just wouldn't obey. The closer we got to the beach, the more anxious I became. I needed to know as soon as possible whether the events of the previous day were real or only imagined. My heart was racing.

I spent about fifteen minutes convincing the rental manager that I was in fact not crazy. Actually I'm not sure I convinced him. He might have given in to my request for another kayak simply because he grew tired of my insistence that he let me go out again. I apologized profusely, signed up for a two-hour rental, and promised him that I would not return late. We shook hands, but his half smile betrayed skepticism.

Katherine had found her spot on the beach. I dragged the boat to where she lay and then stood patiently as she squeezed out nearly half a tube of sunscreen, working it into my shoulders, neck, face, and forehead. I then lathered up my legs and finally donned a swim shirt under the life jacket, at least guaranteeing a lower degree of additional sunburn should I doze off again on the water.

The sea was as calm as the day before, and it took me only a few minutes to launch and paddle out close to the floating flag. Once there I eased up, lay the paddle down, and waited. And waited. I didn't know what else to do, never having summoned a storm by sheer will before. And I wasn't sleepy today. Ironically, after all that had taken place, I had slept like a baby the night before. So what was I to do? How would I get back to my island and the old man?

Again, his parting words rang in my ears: ". . . *you will know what to do. Trust me with the physical journey.*" Trust him? After listening to Katherine and the rental manager, I wasn't even sure that he existed.

I closed my eyes, leaned back in the boat, and folded my hands across my chest. That's when I noticed the absence of the shell necklace. When we left the cottage, I had stashed it in a pocket in my bathing trunks. I worked my hand down inside the boat's cockpit and retrieved the necklace. Placing it around my neck, I cupped the shell in my hands. If the shell possessed any kind of magical power, now was the time for it to act. Again I closed my eyes.

Almost immediately I could sense the sky darkening through my eyelids. The temperature dropped, and the wind picked up. I fought the urge to open my eyes, worried that doing so might trigger some sort of cessation to the dramatic change in weather. As the sea began to roll and the boat began to rock, I clutched the paddle with one hand while holding the shell with the other. Water was sloshing over the gunwales now, and rain was pelting my head. How long did I have to endure this? And did my returning to the island require that I be separated from the kayak again?

"*Don't fight the storm,*" the old man had said, but it took every fiber of my being not to mount some resistance. It was human nature. Still with my eyes closed, I put both hands on the paddle and lifted it high above my head, a crazy demonstration of passivity in the face of nature's fury. Suddenly I felt the wind calm, the rain lighten, and the sea's turbulence diminish. I lowered the paddle to rest across my lap and allowed one eye to squint open. In the distance I could see the distinctive shoreline of my secret island. I opened both eyes now. I could see the dramatic cliffs far off to the south. I turned and looked behind me but saw nothing except endless ocean. I had made it back.

I quickly paddled the few hundred yards to shore, where I beached the boat and dragged it up to rest against a tree. I stuffed the life jacket inside and rested the paddle against the hull. Then I turned around and searched the tree line for the path's opening. About fifty yards away I spotted it and half sprinted toward it. Taking one last glance up and down the beach, and again out at the sea's horizon, I turned and ducked into the jungle.

———

I made quick work of the tunneled forest and soon found myself standing at the old man's door. Abandoning all etiquette or protocol, I pushed open the door and entered, overwhelmed with excitement that all the events of the previous day appeared to be real.

"Good morning!" I yelled into the small living space. I looked around the room. The notepad was right where I had left it on the table. I picked it up and studied my list for a moment. Suddenly I thought of my business partner Tom and wondered what his eight vices would be. I imagined that ours lists would be very similar, if not identical.

I looked up from the pad upon realizing that my loud greeting had gone unacknowledged. Returning the pad back to the table, I walked to the kitchen. The old man was not there. With some hesitation I eased the door to his bedroom open and peered inside. His bed was neatly made, and a stack of books was arranged on a bedside table, a wine glass sitting atop them. The door to a small adjoining bathroom was open, and I could see that he was not there either.

It didn't take a genius to conclude that the old man was not at home. Feeling suddenly troubled by his absence, I went back outside and walked around the house. There was a small garden behind the cottage, a bicycle, and a few fishing poles but no old man. Where could he be? I wondered. Had he abandoned the cottage and left the island? Or, worse, had I merely imagined the events of yesterday?

I continued on around the house. Just before completing the circuit, I came upon another path. It seemed to be a continuation of the beach trail, broken by the meadow. I paused. Might the old man simply be out for a walk? If so, to where did this other path lead? I was pondering these things when I noticed eights stones, neatly stacked atop each other, on one side of the path's opening. The cairn gave me renewed confidence, and I started up the trail.

———

This path was much different than the other leading in from the beach. When I was only a few minutes into my trek, the tall trees ended, and the trail began to climb up rolling hills dotted with low-lying brush. I would arrive at the summit of one hill only to discover that a higher, steeper ascent awaited me on the other side. Finally, nearly out of breath, I crested a bluff and saw what appeared to be the penultimate peak in the distance. Seagulls were circling its summit. They were squawking and flying back and forth to one point in particular, clearly drawn there for some specific reason. I walked a bit further and was just beginning to feel the effects of hiking in thin water shoes when I spotted him. It was the old man. He was throwing something to the seagulls, which they were catching more often than not in mid-flight. When I cupped my hands and yelled, he stopped feeding the gulls and turned to look down at me.

"Well, hey there!" he shouted down from his perch. "You're early! Come on up."

Inspired by the sight of him, I found a last burst of energy and pushed up the final leg of the mountain to arrive at his side. If the climb itself had not stolen my breath, the view at the top took care of that. It was beautiful beyond words. The cliffs stretched far into the distance on either side. White sand beaches far below hugged the base of the mountains, disappearing now and then into lagoons. We were so high up that, while I could see the waves crashing against the shore, I could not hear them.

"Pretty amazing, huh?" said the old man, keenly aware of my awe.

"And then some," I replied.

"It's like this every morning."

I looked at him then. He was studying the horizon. "Wait a minute," I said. "You come up here every morning?"

"Right at sunrise, except for those rare days when the weather doesn't permit. For as long as I've been here on the island. Wouldn't miss a day."

"I had no idea," I stammered.

"Well, of course, how would you? We only just met. . . ."

Lost in a state of wonder, I didn't let him finish. "No, I had no idea that such beauty existed. I mean, I've traveled to places but nowhere like this."

"Yeah, somebody knew what they were doing, didn't they?"

I wasn't sure what he meant, but I agreed all the same. "Yeah, somebody or some force, mother nature, whatever. It's beyond me, that's for sure."

I sat down beside him on the rocky outcropping. We both stared into the distance for a while. He had run out of bread crusts, and the seagulls had settled all around us, as though we were statues in a city park.

"So," I said, suddenly curious. "Every morning, huh? Can I ask why? I mean, I realize that the view alone is pretty arresting, but is there something more?"

The old man looked out across the great expanse of ocean and sky. "To be honest with you, I couldn't make it through the day without first coming up here."

"I don't understand," I replied.

"It gives me balance. Being up here in the morning, before my mind starts to wade into the matters of the day, lays a solid foundation for whatever comes my way."

I was silent, trying to absorb his words. "*Balance*," I half whispered.

"What was that?" The old man strained to hear me. It was easy to forget that he was up there in years, no matter that he was obviously in great shape. I had lost my breath making the climb. It escaped me how he could manage such a feat every morning.

"I was just thinking about what you said about balance. I can't even relate to the word. My life has felt largely *out of balance* for longer than I can remember."

Another few moments of silence ensued. We were enjoying the kind of view that can easily be spoiled by words. Even so the old man had reminded me of yesterday's assignment, and I was anxious to dig deeper into his trove of wisdom. In a way this seemed the perfect place to reveal my second vice.

"Busyness," I said, with no other introduction.

The old man looked at me as if he had missed some transition into another vein of discussion.

"The next vice on my list," I clarified, "back there on the coffee table in your house."

"Oh," he nodded, turning to look back out over the sea again. "I see. Yes, that's a tough one. What brings that to your mind at this moment?"

I thought about his question. It was the kind that one knows the answer to without being able to verbalize it at the moment. "Because," I began slowly, the words still formulating in my mind, "I think that at this moment, in this place, looking out over this magnificent view, I feel whatever is the complete opposite of busy."

The old man nodded. "Yes," he said, "I feel that too. I think it's called tranquility. And it treats busyness the same way as a dolphin treats a shark. The two can't share the same space."

I liked his analogy, and I wondered whether he spoke from experience, so I asked him, "Did you ever find yourself in the grip of busyness?"

"I did, yes, a long time ago, but no more."

"How did you escape it?"

"Well, I started believing a certain truth about man's relation to others and how, if followed, it can free him of that trap to which you allude."

"Tell me about it."

"Of course," he said. "Listen carefully. *He who builds a bridge to those around him will become heir to life's richest peace.*"

"I'm not following you," I said. "I mean, I don't see the connection."

He scanned the vista as if searching for a way to clarify his message. "With few exceptions," he began, "being too busy leads to being self-absorbed. People afflicted with busyness never come up for air. They're always going a hundred miles an hour. They tend to be goal-oriented to the extreme, often to a fault, and they find themselves without any time for relationships, missing out on a deeper level of human interaction that gives us life in the first place. They can't seem to lock in on a good pace, and the pace they settle on often proves unsustainable. They get further and further away from any semblance of balance. Eventually they burn the bridges that connect them to the people around them. From a workplace perspective, people under their charge begin to feel used by them when they are asked to sacrifice for "the good of the team." Even worse, those they love most, friends and family, find it increasingly hard to connect with them on a genuine level. Conversely, the person wise enough to keep those relational bridges open and active enjoys a mutually beneficial two-way lifeline. Cut that connection and you lose a major ingredient of that balance I mentioned."

Even though I didn't want to admit as much, I now understood how over the years my professional drive and ambition had caused me to lose sight of those relationships that I held most dear. In particular I remembered in painful detail an episode involving my daughter Lauren and my mother that jolted me at the time.

My mother was battling cancer, and each week she grew increasingly weaker. I kept telling her to rest and conserve her energy. We would visit her in the assisted-care facility where she lived, and each time she insisted on preparing something for us to eat and making her Southern sweet tea. It got to the point where I was almost tempted to tell her that we wouldn't visit if she was determined to wait on us. But Katherine, in her intuitive way, would point out that caring for her family, for us, was in fact exactly the kind of activity that gave my mother the will to press on. So I did my best to let her serve us and tell myself that Katherine was right. Then there was the matter of the swing.

Behind the facility where my mother lived was a playground for those times when grandchildren came calling. Lauren, who was seven at the time, loved to wander out back and play there. We could see her just fine from the window in the main room of my mother's apartment, but that wasn't enough for my mother. As soon as Lauren headed for the swing, my mother would stand up, excuse herself from the tiny living room where we sat, and walk gingerly out to the playground to sit beside Lauren on that swing. I would start to intercept my mother, worried that she might lose her balance and fall, but Katherine would gently grab my arm and guide me back down to the couch.

"Let her go," she would say. "She knows exactly what she's doing, Jack. It's her choice how she spends the last moments of her life, and if she wants to do that on the swing with Lauren, don't take that away from her."

Katherine and I would sit and watch the two of them through the window. We could see them chatting at times, but mostly they would just swing. They might do that for thirty minutes, even an hour. Lauren would look up now and then to smile at her grandmother. My mother looked down at Lauren and beamed the entire time.

Years later, long after my mother had passed away and Lauren was a young lady, I asked my daughter about those times, wondering whether she even remembered them. She gave me that look as if I had asked the dumbest question in the history of the world.

"Do I remember them? Are you serious, Dad? Don't you realize that the only reason I went outside, walking away from her cookies and delicious tea, was that I knew she would follow me out there? Sitting on that swing with grandmother I still count as one of the sweetest moments of my childhood."

I had to turn away when she said that, my eyes suddenly on the verge of tears, but she wasn't finished. At the time I was traveling a good bit and spending far too much time away from my family. Added Lauren: "It was like there was nowhere else grandmother wanted to be, and no one else she wanted to be with. Just me. I felt so loved by her, Dad. I never will forget those moments."

After I briefly recounted my story to the old man, a longer silence followed. "*Empathy*," he eventually said, this time turning to face me directly and draw me back into the present moment. "Your mother was demonstrating empathy, Legacy Virtue number two, the next of the Great 8, the virtue meant to counter busyness."

"How so?"

"Well," he explained, "those who are too busy become numb to the feelings of those around them. They do not empathize with others because they are so preoccupied with their own objectives. They don't feel, relate, listen, understand. They find it increasingly difficult to enter into another person's situation. They miss what that the other person might have to offer. In a nutshell, they don't empathize."

"Okay," I said, "I'm with you, but what do empathetic people do to counter the distraction of busyness?"

"Empathetic people slow down long enough to value relationships. In a way the ability to empathize is connected to the first virtue, humility. It takes a humble person to be able to set aside his or her own objectives long enough to care about the plight of those around them. People who demonstrate empathy are able to identify with others in the normal ups and downs of life. When someone is struggling, they have the capacity to feel what the other person feels. These are the kinds of people you want around when everything in life isn't perfect, which is pretty much all the time. Sometimes these people don't say much, but they are present, listening, making the effort to understand. You know they have your back in business, in life, in times of prosperity or peril. If something good happens, they can celebrate the event with you without jealousy or envy. Being a person who empathizes isn't easy; it takes patience and commitment. But in the end don't we all want people around us who care more about us as individuals rather than about the bottom line?"

I soaked in his words against the breathtaking backdrop of sea and sun, but he wasn't finished.

"An old friend of mine used to say that 'People don't care how much you know until they know how much you care.' I would propose that the opposite is also true. When you don't care about those around you, either at home or at work, and they sense this, they will care even less about you as a leader. Their loyalty will wane, and that's not a good thing for relationships and certainly not for business."

"I guess you could almost make the case," I interjected, "that empathy makes the work environment not only more enjoyable but also more productive. It might actually *enhance* the bottom line."

"There's no question but that it will," the old man agreed. "You see, Jack, empathetic people are better able to prioritize. They can more quickly discern what has to be done immediately and what can wait. In this way they can be in the present moment with people without compromising effectiveness, without forsaking the bottom line."

"In a word," I said, "it all comes down to maintaining balance."

"Yes, balance."

The sun was rising, and it was becoming difficult to enjoy the prospect before us without squinting. We both sensed the approaching end of our time together high atop the bluff. We both stood, sensing that the time had arrived to say goodbye to the moment.

As we did so, the old man put his hand on my shoulder with an almost fatherly touch that froze me in my tracks. "One question," he said.

"Sure."

"In all these years have you been able to forgive yourself?"

I looked in his eyes and could tell immediately what it was to which he was referring. "You mean Lauren, don't you?"

He nodded, his eyes softening in empathy.

I hesitated. I think that over the years I had chosen to bury the guilt and remorse whenever I felt them creeping up. Our conversation this morning had no doubt unearthed some hidden but painful scars that I had worked hard to conceal. "I don't know. I guess that I haven't thought about it in those terms before, or at least in quite a long while. If nothing else, I'm trying to make up for it. I have grandchildren now, and I'm trying hard not to repeat the same mistakes I made with my own children."

"Well," he said, "I think that you should forgive yourself. Empathy starts with oneself. If you can't understand and come to a peaceful agreement with your own life past, present, and future, you will find it nearly impossible to establish that zone of trust with others."

I knew almost instinctively that the old man was right. "I will try," I said. "I will really try."

"Good," he said. "Now let's get off this mountain and back down to my home. I want to make you one of my famous omelets."

I smiled at his claim. "Oh yeah? And what makes them so famous?"

"They're the only ones on the island."

I laughed. Then we turned together and began to pick our way down the trail, the morning sun at our backs.

7

Praus

"Come on, boy," the soldier said. "Let's do this the easy way."

The man was physically impressive. He stood well over six feet, broad-shouldered and barrel-chested, his soft words seemingly at odds with his chiseled features. Lifting the horse's reins, he opened the gate, swung it wide, and led him out. As the two made their way out into the light, the soldier assessed the massive beast. Eighteen and a half hands, he thought to himself, perhaps nineteen, easily the largest stallion in camp. If broken properly, the steed could mean the difference between a battle won or lost. Conversely, if the animal proved too stubborn and unteachable, he would be good for nothing more than breeding, and in times of war even that was not promised.

The descent proved trickier than I imagined. On the way up I hadn't noticed how much loose gravel covered the trail. I slowed my pace in an effort to descend safely. The old man, meanwhile, bounded ahead of me. I tried to keep up with him, but he veered out of sight around a bend in the trail. His morning ritual of quiet reflection had apparently produced a well of surplus energy.

Suddenly I heard a muffled cry in the distance. I quickened my pace while simultaneously trying to keep my balance. I lowered my body to get more leverage, steadying myself against boulders and reaching out for the low-lying brush that was slowly giving way to taller vegetation. Finally I rounded a thick stand of mango trees and saw the old man lying on the ground and clutching his leg.

"Are you alright?" I said. "What happened?"

To my surprise he started to laugh. "Well," he said, chuckling as he sat up, "what happened is that I forgot how old I am."

I knelt down beside him and tried to assess the injury. Then I reached down to help him up. He stood, put weight on the leg and immediately sat back down.

"Wow," he said. "That really hurts. I think I twisted my ankle pretty good."

"You must have hit some of that loose gravel," I surmised.

"That and I got distracted."

"Distracted?"

"I was thinking about our breakfast and whether I had enough eggs to make your omelet."

"Do you want me to go for help?" I said, realizing as soon as the words left my mouth how silly they were.

"Ha! The only help around here is you. Thank goodness I'm not alone today. All the times I've gone up and down this hill without incident! At least you're here on the one day I fall."

I helped him up again, and this time he draped his arm around my shoulder, lifted his bad ankle, and we slowly hobbled down the trail together. It took us a good half an hour to make it back to the cottage. Once inside, I directed him to the couch where he lay down, removed his shoe, and propped his leg up on the coffee table, trying to regulate the blood flow. The ankle had already begun to swell. At his direction I fetched a bag of ice from the freezer that he draped across the ankle.

"Well darn," he said. "I guess that the omelet will have to wait until another day. I'm pretty helpless at this point."

I stood looking down at him. I was undeniably hungry, and he had to be as well after the long hike up and back.

"Have you ever had a sailboat egg?" I asked.

"A what?"

"A sailboat egg. Ever heard of one? It was my mother's breakfast specialty when we were kids. We could have eaten them every morning if she had let us."

"No," the old man admitted, "can't say that I ever have. It sounds intriguing and very Caribbean."

"Oh no," I replied. "There's nothing Caribbean about it. It's actually just a simple Southern treat."

"What's required?" the old man asked.

"Not much," I answered, "just some bread, a few eggs, and a frying pan."

"Those I can provide."

I slapped my hands together. "Okay then. I'll be the chef this morning. Now just direct me to my supplies."

"Well, the first thing you'll need to do is to go out back and fetch a few fresh eggs. Mother Goose is my main egg provider. She's in the coop on the far left. She usually has a few large ones ready by this time of the morning. She's friendly enough. Just reach in, move her gently off to the side, and steal her treasures. She'll forgive you and get right back to making more."

"Okay," I said, realizing that this wasn't going to be like the typical run to the nearest grocery store. "Will do."

I did as he said, and Mother Goose complied. I was back inside with eight large eggs in a minute's time. There it was again, the number eight! I went to the tiny kitchen and placed them on the counter.

"The bread is in that silver tin beside the fridge," the old man yelled from the couch. "A frying pan is in the big cabinet directly beneath it."

I found everything, clicked on the gas stove, heated the pan, and greased it with half a stick of butter I found in the fridge. A sailboat egg was about the simplest thing that one not prone to cooking anything other than burgers and hot dogs on a grill could manage to make. I can't say exactly how old I was when I first tasted them as a child, but sailboat eggs were an integral part of our family history. They came as naturally to a

Saturday morning as cartoons. You simply cut a hole in the middle of a slice of bread, toasted it in the pan, and poured an egg in the center. Give it half a minute and then flip it over. After another minute the concoction was done. Voilà! You had a white sail billowing out of the boat fashioned by the bread.

Seeing a French press on the counter, I ground some coffee beans and made a full pot for the two of us to share. I placed four of the eggs in the fridge and cooked the rest. Then I carried everything over to the couch on a tray and set it down before us. I noticed the notepad still sitting there from yesterday, which seemed like an eternity ago. In less than five minutes we downed all four sailboats and nearly all of the coffee.

"Wow," the old man said, licking his fingertips. "That was absolutely delicious. Well done, my friend."

"All credit to my mother. I only wish you could have sampled hers."

My host's leg was still elevated, and the swelling was pretty severe. I had replaced the ice already, and it looked as though he was about due for a fresh batch.

"That's a nasty ankle sprain," I said. "I wonder whether we need to figure out how to get you off the island and see somebody about it."

"Heavens no," he said, laughing out loud. "I've suffered much worse and lived to see another day. I'll be okay. I should have been paying better attention while coming down the trail. Took the path for granted, I guess, and got distracted."

There was that word again—*distracted*. I looked down at the notepad and then into the old man's eyes. "Have you been reading my notes from yesterday?" I inquired.

The old man shook his head, but I wasn't sure whether he meant "no" or just didn't understand my question.

"It's not a big deal," I added. "After all, I'm eventually going to share all of them with you. I just wondered whether maybe you skipped ahead."

"No, no," the old man was quick to say. "What makes you ask that?"

"Well, you keep using the word 'distracted.'"

"It just seemed to fit," he explained. "I was coming down the trail and started thinking about what to cook for breakfast, wondering whether Mother Goose would have enough eggs for me to make my signature omelet. I got distracted and lost my focus."

I reached over to the where the notepad lay and slowly turned it around so that the old man could read what I had written there. Toward the top of the page were the words "egotism" and "busyness," then a handful of other words I had jotted down but later lined through in favor of a third vice.

The old man looked at the page and smiled. "I see," he said. "That's the next one on your list. No wonder you were caught off guard by my use of the word, but tell me more. What exactly do you mean by your use of the word?"

I drained the last of my coffee and sat back in the chair. "I guess it just seems that there is so much information and data coming my way every day. It doesn't seem to stop. It's like . . . noise pollution. And there is so much of it that it's hard to actually hear anything."

The old man was nodding.

"Out here, okay, not so much, but back there. . . . I mean, it's so heavy at times that I almost become paralyzed. And I find it hard to leave all that noise behind at work. It's almost impossible to keep it from following me home. I'll find myself riding in the car with Katherine, and we're having a conversation, maybe even a truly meaningful one, and without meaning for it to happen my mind drifts away to something going on at work or maybe even to something trivial, something that doesn't contribute much to my life at all, like sports or a movie I recently saw. Then Katherine's voice will suddenly bring me back. "Where did you just go?" she'll ask me. Then I'll feel wracked with guilt and can't refocus enough to find my way back into the conversation with her."

The old man put his coffee cup down and leaned back into the couch. I saw him grimace and realized that it had been a while since I changed the ice.

"Are you okay?" I asked. "Is it time for fresh ice?"

"No, I'm fine," he half lied. "Just needed to reposition the leg. Go on. I'm listening."

Satisfied that he was okay, I continued. "I mean, call me old-fashioned, but I can remember back before we had personal computers, cell phones, and fax machines. Katherine and I were at different colleges, and we mailed letters to each other. Whenever I received one of hers, I was so excited. I would find a quiet place where no one could bother me, and then I would open her letter and read it slowly before tucking it away in a safe place. Later I would pull it out again and reread it several times. Of course we were in love, and I was highly motivated, but I would dwell on each of her words. They were precious and so were the moments spent reading them."

I paused again, caught up in my self-induced nostalgia.

"Now, of course, we have email, text messaging, Facebook, Twitter. I hate to admit it, but there are times when I get an email from Katherine and I ignore it because a dozen others, usually business-related, are begging for my attention. When I finally take the time to read her message, I don't have the time to answer as thoughtfully as I know I should."

The old man stopped me at this point. "You know, Jack, you're preaching to the choir here. Though I must admit I am not familiar with all of your technological terms, I get your point. After all, I've been around quite a while. I remember when the only way to communicate with someone you cared about was to go to meet with them face to face, no matter the distance or the obstacles that stood in your way."

Now I was the one nodding. "We have all these amazing modern inventions," I remarked, "but you have to wonder whether, while supposedly saving us time, they haven't stolen something away from us more precious than time."

"Don't beat yourself up, Jack. This happens to everyone. I'm sure Katherine understands that."

"Yeah, she says she does, but that doesn't excuse me from letting it happen." I looked down then, feeling a bit ashamed. Maybe I was being a bit too honest. "I'm afraid this is one vice that no virtue can handle. As you said, this happens to everyone."

"Yes, it does, but you're wrong in supposing that there's no answer. It starts, though, by realizing the heart of the problem. It isn't about those things that distract you. It's about you and the license you've given those things."

"What do you mean?" I said. "What license?"

He looked me straight in the eye while speaking his next words. "It seems, Jack, that you've lost your ability to tame your power and instead are giving it away to those things that distract you most."

"I have power? What power?"

"We all have power," the old man said with conviction, "but it's what we do with that power that makes all the difference in life."

"I want to understand," I said. "Help me understand."

"Of course. Listen carefully."

"I'm all ears. For once, at least, I'm not distracted."

He smiled at my half-hearted attempt to lighten the conversation before saying, *"Power tamed gives way to mastery of all that surrounds you."*

"'Power tamed'?" I repeated.

"That's right. Power tamed." He hesitated before continuing. "Did you ever study any Greek by chance?"

"No," I answered. "I took Spanish in high school and for a year in college, but to be honest I don't remember much of it, only a few phrases. Foreign languages were never my strong suit."

"Well, there is a Greek word, *praus*, that signifies a war horse."

„A war horse?"

"That's right. *Praus* is the word the ancient Greeks used to describe a stellar war horse. You couldn't take just any horse, even a well trained one, into battle. It had to be a horse that would obey instantly its rider's commands, no matter the circumstances. At the height of battle, in the midst of chaos and confusion, a soldier had to know that his horse would remain calm and do exactly as he directed. He could only count on a horse that had tamed its power, a horse that was strong but not prone to release that power until it was absolutely needed."

"Okay," I interrupted, "but what's the connection to the vice of distraction?"

"The only kind of horse that could meet that standard was one completely focused, one hundred percent at the ready. Only then could it be trusted to perform at the blink of an eye."

"I still don't follow you."

"The next Legacy Virtue," said the old man, "number three, the state of mind in which one has to be in order to handle the realities of war—*attentiveness*."

"Attentiveness?" I echoed skeptically. "That seems too simple."

"Most of the great virtues *are* simple," he replied, "but humankind can't seem to accept that fact. It's kind of like not being able to see the forest for the trees. As you said, there's a steady stream of information flowing your way, right? On a daily basis, I mean."

I nodded. "More like hourly."

"But how much are you really listening? The real challenge in life and in business is to prioritize information based on its value to the mission at hand. In order to do that, one has to practice attentiveness. And being consistently attentive is not easy. Focused, attentive listening is a skill developed over time. It does not occur naturally. Sometimes you just have to get away from the day-to-day battle, ironically, so you that you will be ready for the *next* battle."

I thought about our time up on the bluff and the fact that the old man went up there every day. "Your morning ritual overlooking the sea," I said, verbalizing my thought.

"Exactly. That certainly helps me to fight distraction, even if I clearly failed in that department coming down this morning."

We both smiled.

"Solitude is a key ingredient in developing the virtue of attentiveness," he continued. "Leaders of any organization, team, or cause, if they want to maximize their effectiveness, *must* carve out blocks of time for undistracted moments away from the task at hand."

I reflected for a moment on our time together atop the cliff. There was no doubt that it had left me refreshed and filled with a sense of peace, but another reality was gnawing at me. "There is no mountaintop with a view of the ocean in the suburbs of Atlanta," I said, "no place to which I can repair in order to get away from normative distractions."

"Fair enough," the old man admitted, "but solitude is not so much about a physical experience. It takes more effort, of course, but one can disconnect from that clutter without traveling across an ocean. It's much more about an internal action of pulling away. Solitude can take place in the midst of chaos if one makes a habit of it and learns how to block out that noise and clutter. Really Jack, it's more about what you choose *not* to let in than about what's actually out there."

"Give me some examples," I said, my mind open to his proposal but still not quite grasping its applications.

"Well, again, it's simple things, but you have to commit to practicing them. You might have to get up a little earlier. Close your eyes during the day more. Turn off your cell phone. Shut down the computer. Say no to everyone except your family. Listen to more music that doesn't have lyrics. Read more things that have nothing to do with work. Ignore sports for a while. Get outside regardless of the weather. Travel to quiet places."

Suddenly I realized that I was nodding without knowing it. I instinctively knew that what he was saying was exactly what I needed to hear. He wasn't finished, however.

"In short, Jack, you need to put yourself in a posture of listening to your family, to your clients, to your business partners, and to yourself."

Again I was nodding throughout his wise counsel.

"At the end of the day, if you aren't hearing those with and for whom you work, they will sense it, and your business will suffer. People are everything in business. That can sometimes be forgotten. If you stop listening to them, your business will gradually die. Defeat distraction by being attentive. Control the power you have been given. Don't give it away to anyone or anything. Rule it; don't let it rule you. Allow it to *free* you so that you can be all you were meant to be in life and work."

The old man fell silent. I was too while absorbing his words. Suddenly I wished that Tom and Katherine were there beside me to hear what the old man had been saying. Thinking of Katherine caused me to check my watch. It was almost noon. andI had promised to be back in two hours. If I didn't leave right away, I couldn't keep that promise.

"I need to go," I said.

The old man nodded.

"Will you be okay?" I asked, looking down at his leg.

"Oh, this old thing?" he said, masking some pain. "Heck, it's practically healed already. I'll be up and walking by the time you reach the beach."

"Is it okay if I come back again tomorrow?" I queried.

The old man cracked a smile. "I had hoped for nothing less. I'm really enjoying your company."

"Yeah, me too. I hope that Katherine will let me come."

The ice pack was drooping over the old man's ankle now, and I didn't even ask whether he wanted me to get him a fresh bag. I took the melted ice along with the dirty dishes to the kitchen. where I tidied up. Then I refilled the ice bag and placed it over the old man's sprained ankle.

"Jack?" the old man said while I was exiting from the cabin.

"Yes?"

"About today. Thanks. Not sure how I would have made it down that hill without you."

I smiled. "Of course. Glad I could help in some way, a very small return on all the help you've already given me." With that acknowledgment I left the cottage.

8

The Dance

They stood facing one another in the middle of the crudely con-
structed corral at the edge of camp. An invisible wall stood be-
tween them. The great horse pawed at the ground and looked
everywhere except directly into the soldier's eyes. The man spoke
in firm yet soft tones. He held the reins in one hand and at-
tempted to stroke the stallion's cheek with the other. The horse
would have none of it. Each time he jerked his head upward,
pulling at the reins and away from the soldier's hand. The man
gave up and began to walk the horse in a circle at the outer edge
of the corral. After a few steps the horse jerked to a stop, pawing
harder at the ground, lowering and lifting his head, trying to
pull the reins from the soldier's grasp. About halfway around the
corral, instead of stopping, the horse changed his tactic. Lowering
his muzzle and breaking into a gallop, the stallion succeeded in
freeing himself from the man's grip. He crossed to the corral's far
side but once there could only stop at the high rail. He turned once
again to face the soldier, who seemed to be not the least surprised.
Sighing and with a hint of impatience, the man walked toward
the horse.

My journey back to Katherine was relatively uneventful. By now I
had become used to storms suddenly arising, to roiling seas and

dark thunder clouds besieging my tiny vessel. I arrived back on the beach and stood in front of the rental hut well before my allotted two hours, the dimension of time clearly something out of the ordinary on the hidden island. My early return elicited a look of surprise from the rental manager.

Katherine and I then headed back to our bungalow's back patio to enjoy some mid-day cocktails. Our conversation was light and sporadic. Instead of talking too much, we chose to marvel at the sea not far away. I was worried that she might ask questions about my time on the water, but I accepted her choice to be silent.

I finally decided that now was a good moment for confession. "I want to apologize," I said.

"Apologize?" she repeated. "For what, Jack? You haven't done anything."

"Don't let me off so easy," I countered. "It's more about what I haven't done."

"What do you mean?"

"Well, I've left you twice now. I fell asleep early last night and awoke with kayaking again on my mind. I don't feel that I've given much of myself to you since we arrived."

"I meant what I said before: this vacation is for both of us, and I don't want to limit whatever it is you need to do and experience while we are here. When we get on that plane home in a few days, I want you to feel as though you maximized your time here."

"Okay then," I said. "Tonight I want to take you to the nicest restaurant on the island. I want to share a bottle of the best wine with you, and if that doesn't knock us out, I want to wrap my arm around your waist and dance with you as we haven't danced since the day we married."

"Okay," she agreed. "I second all of that. One question, though."

"Shoot."

"Do we really have to wait until after dinner?"

Later we enjoyed appetizers and cocktails before ordering our main courses. Just before they arrived on the terrace where we were sitting, the western sky exploded into brilliant oranges, reds, and yellows. I couldn't help but think of the view atop the ridge that same morning. For the second time in the same day, I watched amazed. Katherine seemed to sense the majesty of the moment as well, and we both sat paralyzed for several minutes, jarred back to the present only when the waiter placed our entrees on the table in front of us.

When we couldn't eat another bite, we made our way down to the beachside dance floor. Katherine and I took advantage of the slower sets. We laughed when we accidentally stepped on one another's toes or mistimed a move we would have executed easily thirty years earlier. During one such moment, when I almost tripped her, Katherine stepped back and accidentally bumped into another couple. They were curiously mismatched, one of the young, energetic professional dancers in her island costume dancing with a man who appeared old enough to be her grandfather. The short-brimmed fedora atop his head seemed a bit out of place on the dance floor, but he moved rather elegantly around the parquet for someone his age. When Katherine made contact, she immediately apologized, at which the older gentleman turned to confront us. When I saw his face, I nearly choked and collapsed. It wasn't just any old man; it was *the* old man!

"No worries at all," he said to Katherine, and then had to reach out and steady her because in my momentary state of disbelief my arm came off her waist. He stopped her fall and guided her back into my embrace, at the same time giving me a slight wink.

I stared back at him, dumbfounded. It took prompting by Katherine to bring me out of my temporary inattention.

"*Honey,*" she said, cocking her head sideways with a hint of embarrassment in her voice. Katherine did not seem to notice what I thought to be obvious similarities between his features and mine. Apparently the fedora was serving as a cover. I stared a moment longer before I realized that she was trying to tell me something.

"Oh, yes . . . of course, "I stammered. "Thank you so much. Sorry . . . about . . . that."

"Don't think of it for another moment," the old man said. "My clumsy feet likely blundered into your space. It's been quite some time since I danced."

"Well, it doesn't appear that way," Katherine was quick to reply. "You sure look like you know what you're doing."

"Boy, does he," his dance partner said. "He moves better than men half his age."

"Hey, wait a minute," the old man protested, a wry smile on his face. "That was uncalled for."

His partner grinned and put her arm around his neck. "Oh come on now, Jack," she said coyly. "That was a compliment two times over."

"Jack?" Katherine half exclaimed. "What a coincidence! That's my husband's name."

Again the old man looked at me as if to say, *Well, what name did you expect me to use?*

"Listen," remarked the young woman. "Are we all going to stand here in the middle of the dance floor carrying on a conversation or get back to dancing? I'd prefer the latter."

"Oh gosh, I'm so sorry," Katherine replied. "Of course, of course! Carry on. Sorry we disturbed you."

The young woman nodded, and the old man tipped his hat and executed a subtle bow. As he did, he caught me staring at his ankle, the same one that was swollen six hours earlier. He gave me one last glance—I could swear he was almost laughing—as they turned away.

Katherine and I finished dancing to the song, and then I told her I needed a break. And maybe another drink. My feet were tired, but more than that a million questions were running through my head. Why had the old man come to the island? How did he get here? Did he notice us on the dance floor and seek out our encounter? Was there something he had come to tell me? How would he get back to his island? And how in the world was he able to dance on that ankle?

Katherine and I found an empty table a dozen feet back from the surf right at the edge of a grove of mango trees. A waitress brought us drinks, and we relaxed by the water's edge. The moon was full in the Caribbean sky, and the stars were out in all their glory. I kept glancing around to see where the old man was, but there were many couples still on the dance floor, and he must have been lost in the sea of bodies.

Katherine broke the silence. "He was quite charming, don't you think?"

"Who?" I played dumb.

"That older gentleman. I mean, in an endearing, grandfatherly kind of way."

"Um, yeah, I guess so. I wasn't really paying much attention."

"Do you think he just met that woman or that they were, you know, together?"

"Hah!" I laughed. "Together? Gosh, no. He's not even from here," I said without thinking.

Katherine looked at me. "What do you mean he's not from here? How would you know? Have you met him before?"

I was caught. I certainly didn't want to lie to my wife, but I also was not ready to divulge my short history with the old man, the secret island, and all that came with it.

I collected myself. "I mean, no one is from here, right, except the staff? I'm sure he's a visitor just like us. She was one of the dancers from the show earlier. I imagine they both wanted to dance and just ended up together."

That seemed to satisfy Katherine. "He just seemed, I don't know, almost chivalrous. Maybe that's what I mean, more than charming. Kind. Genuinely kind. You don't see that so much anymore," she said.

We both fell silent again and sipped our drinks. We remained that way for several minutes before our silence was interrupted by a familiar voice. The old man had walked up quietly and now stood right beside our table.

"Well, hello again," he said, startling both of us.

"Oh goodness," remarked Katherine.

"Sorry if I frightened you."

"No, it's okay. Please." She motioned to one of the empty chairs at our table. "Won't you join us?"

"Why, I'd love to," replied the old man. He looked at me. "Do you mind?"

I stared up at him, wondering what he was up to. "Of course not," I half lied. "Please join us."

He sat down, and the shadows of the mango trees, coupled with his fedora, conveniently concealed his facial features. Something told me that this was intentional on his part, his way of ensuring that Katherine wouldn't notice how much he looked like her husband.

"How's the wine?" asked the old man.

"The merlot's not bad," Katherine said. "I didn't catch the brand, but it's nice. Very dry, which I prefer."

"Great," he said, then motioned to a nearby waitress. When she approached, he asked for a bottle of whatever it was that Katherine was drinking.

"I'd consider it an honor if you'd allow me to replenish your glasses," he said.

"Oh, no thanks," Katherine said, covering the top of her glass with her palm. "You're very kind, but I've had my quota for the night."

"*I'll* have more," I commented, suddenly determined to do whatever it took to keep the old man in our company. I wanted to find out why he was here.

"Wonderful," he said, nodding at the waitress.

"Again, so kind of you," Katherine remarked. She then added, "You're quite the dancer."

"Oh that?" he replied, glancing back at the dance floor. "It's a miracle I didn't trip over myself and take others out in the process. I had a pretty skilled partner."

"Well, you're humility is noble," Katherine said, "but not quite honest. I'd say that you were doing a good job of holding your own out there."

"You two seemed to know how to carve up a floor pretty well your-selves. And more than that, if I may say so, you looked like a pair who enjoy being together. It was noticeable. Almost a glow."

Katherine looked over at me and smiled. "Well, yes, you *can* say it, and once again you are very kind. That means a lot, doesn't it, honey?" She was prompting me again.

"Yes, yes," I blurted. "Very kind. Thanks for saying that."

"So," Katherine asked, "where are you from?"

"Oh, not so far from here. A small place really. I doubt you've heard of it. How about you folks?"

Nice, I thought. It was an honest but clever answer, leading Katherine away from any follow-up inquiry.

"The U.S. Just outside Atlanta," Katherine answered. "And that feels a world away from here right now. It's going to be hard to get on that plane in a few days."

The waitress delivered the wine and poured a glass for the old man and myself. Katherine reconsidered and accepted a splash. The old man initiated a toast, and we all leaned toward the table's center to tap glasses.

"To new friends brought together beneath a magical sky," he said.

"Agreed," said Katherine, and I nodded as well. "Too perfect to be an accident," Katherine added.

"How do you mean?" the old man asked, putting down his glass.

Caught off guard, Katherine lowered her glass, studied the wine for a moment, and then returned the old man's gaze. "Well, I just think it's too much to believe that such beauty"—she raised her glass toward the star-filled skies—"could be happenstance. It seems to me that all great art and natural wonders are fashioned by the hands of a creator, whether human or heavenly."

"You mean God?" said the old man.

Katherine studied the brilliant expanse of night sky above us. I could tell that she was taking his question seriously, and I sensed that the old man might be in for one of my wife's sporadic soliloquies of personal conviction.

"Maybe," she said. "It's just hard for me to accept that all this"—she paused again and looked up, as if searching the heavens for answers—"is all some kind of colossal accident. That beauty like this can just occur. That I would find a man I love the way I do Jack just because of chance. That I would be given children just because I had a fertile womb."

Katherine was on a roll, and even I was caught up in her spontaneous articulation.

She continued, "I don't judge others for thinking differently. Heck, maybe I'm too simple of mind. Maybe thinking as I do helps me sleep at night, I don't know. But my mind and my heart give credit for all that surrounds us, and on that level I can be at peace, even if I'm not certain to whom I owe this debt."

The old man looked at Katherine a moment longer, then at me. I just shrugged my shoulders as if to say, *You're on your own here*.

"Wow," he said. "That was profound."

Katherine blushed. "Sorry," she replied, smiling. "I'm afraid I got a little carried away. I warned you that I'd had enough wine already."

The old man put his hand to his chest. "I accept full blame," he said. "That was as eloquent as the night sky."

Katherine peered again into her wine glass. "I can't even finish what little you poured me," she said. "That's a sign, I believe."

"A sign?" queried the old man, wondering whether another metaphysical reflection was coming.

"Yes," said Katherine, "a sign that it's time for this lady to head for bed."

"Are you sure, honey?" I piped up, with a touch of insincerity. In truth I was anxious to have the old man to myself. I had a load of questions I was dying to ask him.

"I'm sure," she answered. "I've danced too much, eaten too much, drunk too much, and now, I fear, talked too much."

When she stood, the old man and I joined her.

"Besides," Katherine said. "You, Jack, have been entirely too quiet in this threesome, and I suspect that you and this charming gentleman have more in common than you might think. Maybe you can discuss what brought you both here to the island. Whatever isn't confidential I'll be interested to learn in the morning."

The old man took Katherine's hand, kissed it gently and wished her goodnight. "It was a great pleasure to meet you, Madame. I feel as though I've known you for years, not hours."

"My pleasure is equal, if not greater," answered Katherine. "Now don't keep my Jack up too late."

She kissed the old man gently on the check and left us by the shore. We both stood in silence as she climbed the stairs leading away from the sand and crested the bluff in the direction of the restaurant.

"Well, well," the old man said, breaking the spell. "Now I understand why you wanted me to meet her so badly. What a gem of a woman." He gave me a fatherly jab in the shoulder. "You, my friend, are clearly married up."

Once Katherine was completely out of sight, I turned to face him. "You have a lot of explaining to do," I said.

He laughed. "Ha! I guess it's a good thing I ordered a full bottle of wine."

We returned to our chairs. The old man filled our glasses, and I launched in.

"What about your ankle?" I said. "I was worried that you wouldn't be able to stand, let alone walk. And never would I have dreamed you could glide around a dance floor like that!"

"Well, what can I say? The body is an amazing organism. Surprises us all the time. I have a history of quick recovery. Besides, I kept thinking about your desire that I meet Katherine. Not knowing how many more chances I'd have left, I figured I'd come on over to your island and see whether perhaps I might bump into you two. Little did I know that you'd bump into me first!"

"You expect me to buy all of that?"

"Jack, if there is one thing I've always been with you, it's honest. There are details that are unimportant for you at this time. Remember, you have to trust me. So far, when you've done that, I think things have worked out pretty well, don't you?"

"I can't argue with you there," I admitted, "but my mind still wants more explanation, more details. How did you get here? How will you return? Will you spend the night here? Do you need a place to stay?"

"My friend, you are too kind, but rest assured that I'm at home on this island as much as I am on mine. I am grateful for your concern, but I'd rather you just enjoy this magnificent sky and this delightful wine. I'm sure that we can find more interesting things to chat about than the details of my coming and going."

I sipped my wine, not so sure that I agreed with him. "Like what?" I asked, a little perturbed at how he kept shifting the conversation.

He studied the sky and sipped his merlot. "Well, how about number four on your list? Something tells me that our time is drawing nigh, that you'll be leaving the island soon. I thought that perhaps we could address the next vice on your list."

"I like the idea," I confessed, "but I can't remember what the next entry is."

"Fortunately," said the old man, "I was optimistic that we'd see each other here." He reached into his pocket and produced the list, folded neatly, and handed it to me.

"Optimism indeed," I said. "Something tells me that you operate on the basis of a lot more than mere optimism."

I unfolded the list and lay it across my lap. There was just enough moonlight for me to make out the words. My eyes drifted down past egotism, busyness, and distraction to my fourth item.

"Oh yes," I said. "In terms of ranking this could easily be number one for me, though I hate to admit it."

"I'm ready," replied the old man.

"Greed."

The old man took another sip of wine. "You mean like when someone is overzealous for more information than they really need?" He lowered his eyes in my direction, clearly poking fun at my litany of questions earlier regarding his presence on the island.

"Very funny," I said. "No, more like that seemingly endless struggle we capitalists face everyday between much and too much. It involves an inner battle to balance ambition and drive with justice and fairness."

The old man nodded. "It's a balance that is hard to strike when you've been taught since childhood that more is better."

"Exactly!" I exclaimed. "So you know what I'm talking about?"

"I'm well versed in American culture, you might say. Besides, Western culture has pretty much blanketed the world by now, so I wouldn't say that greed is unique to Americans."

"Good point," I said.

"So tell me more about that battle for balance," the old man probed.

"Ha!" I laughed. "The truth is that it's not much of a battle at all. The side of justice and fairness rarely stands a chance. I guess maybe you can blame it on human nature, but I'm sure you will tell me that's a copout."

"Yes," he said, "it is."

"Well, call me guilty. I confess, but you can't blame me for where I was born. And in truth, regardless of some of its flaws, a capitalistic society, and mine in particular, provides a relatively fair framework for quality of life and the pursuit of happiness."

The old man leaned forward and topped off his wine. He glanced up at me, but I waved him off. "No thanks," I said. "I want to be as clear-minded as possible to discuss this subject."

"Fair enough," the old man said. "I hope that you forgive me if I indulge a bit. They say that red wine is good for one recovering from an injury to the lower extremities."

"Oh really?" I said. "And who exactly are *they*?"

He didn't miss a beat. "The capitalists who own the wineries and the companies who sell their product to the public."

We both laughed. "So what do you think about my point a moment ago?" I asked. "Am I right?"

"I would tend to agree with you that capitalism is the best global business structure. For the most part everyone can pursue his or her dreams. But

I also agree with you that human nature has the uncanny ability to take over and leave things horribly out of balance. And that's when greed too often raises its ugly head. When that happens, greed can quickly, if subliminally, lead to lawlessness and deeply selfish individualism that ignores the dictates of reason, fairness, and compassion. At that point capitalism has gone astray."

I could find no fault with anything he was saying.

"There's one other thing, though."

"What's that?"

"As I said before, greed is not something unique to Western societies. I've observed it at work in Eastern cultures among socialists, autocrats, and even, sad to say, within theocracies, and not just in this era either. The bottom line is that you're talking about a disease that runs rampant all over the world and all down through history."

„So it's a matter of human nature?"

"Yes, I think so," he agreed. "The problem is that greed sacrifices principle on the altar of expedience."

"We humans tend to want everything we long for now."

"Bingo. The plague of instant gratification. And, even worse, the willingness to keep steering in one direction at the expense of others, of their welfare and well-being, be it co-workers, clients, friends, or, at times, even family."

I was looking away from him now, out toward the sea's dark horizon illuminated only by the moon hovering high overhead. I wasn't recalling specific examples, but I knew immediately that I was guilty of many and perhaps all of those things to which he had alluded. I had hurt people in each of the groups he mentioned, blinded by my own desire to "advance" in my career. As I studied the surface of the dark ocean, I felt a wave of remorse wash over my soul.

Finally I spoke. "It seems that we have painted a pretty hopeless picture."

"Not so fast," the old man cautioned. "Again, as I said before, it's only once you understand the disease, what we are calling a vice, that you can be open to its cure."

"Okay, then. Enlighten me."

The old man leaned forward. "It's about hunger."

"How do you mean?"

"The way out is about understanding what you hunger for and why."

"I'm trying to stay with you, but I think I'm getting a little lost."

"Listen carefully."

"All I can hear is the lapping of the ocean and your voice."

"Good. Then I think you're ready."

The old man looked hard into my eyes. "*Seek what's noble and just, resisting the urge toward vain accumulation of that which is perishable, and your appetite will be satisfied by overwhelming abundance.*"

"Tell me more."

"Why don't you tell me?" he said. "What are the opposite values of those who crave the noble, the honorable, and the just?"

"The big three," I said without hesitation, remembering a psychology class I took decades ago. "Money, sex, and power."

"Right. It's universal. And the underlying vice that leads to such pursuits is greed. As you so correctly articulated, greed is focused on personal gain to the exclusion of others. Greed is different, mind you, than what I would call mutually shared self-interest."

"Can you explain that more?"

"Of course. Being motivated by the *collective* interests of an organization to accomplish great things is a good thing, and when that atmosphere exists people are typically willing to offer their collective gifts to fulfill the mission. When greed kicks in, however, the organization suffers. Greed suggests that agreements are made to be broken. Greed entices people to cut secret, under-the-table deals. Greedy people often claim to be working on a "win-win" basis, but the blindness of greed so distorts perception of the "win-win" philosophy that their claim proves to be nothing more than smoke and mirrors. In reality it's only about *their* individual "win." It is startling to me how so many people in business are blinded by greed."

I knew all too well what he was saying. I had seen all shades of ugliness when it came to how off-course a business could veer when those behind a venture allowed themselves to be seduced by greed.

"So," I said with a heavy sigh. "what is the antidote? Is there one?"

The old man smiled. "There is *always* an antidote, Jack. That is the beauty of the Great 8. Legacy Virtue number four," he began. "Accountability."

I thought about this for a moment. It seemed too simple, too elementary.

He sensed my dubiety before I even spoke. "Yeah, I know," he said. "You're thinking it can't be that easy, that black and white."

I nodded.

"Well, why not? Most answers to what ails humanity, whether personally or professionally, tend to be pretty simple, but somehow we humans manage to complicate things to the point where we can't see the forest for the trees."

It was hard to argue with him on this point.

"You see, Jack, accountability counteracts the vice of greed. Accountability means doing business the way it ought to be done, with high ethical standards. It's doing the right thing in the right way with the right motives."

"Of course, you're right," I said. "Few people would disagree with you. The problem is that I rarely see such values and standards enforced in the business world."

"Exactly," the old man exclaimed, "which is precisely why people and organizations must commit to building a *culture* of accountability. This is crucial if you want to achieve prolonged, consistent success. I mean, let's face it: it's relatively easy in a moment of inspiration to say that you are going to do something, but when the moment passes it's just as easy to follow through on a commitment. You have to be careful about what you say and then careful about doing what you say you are going to do. Everyone maintains that business is all about relationships, but these same people will say they are going to do something and then renege, unaware of how that behavior undermines a strong relationship. In the end that kind of behavior will doom a business. Conversely, if you create an environment where accountability is routinely practiced, you inevitably will set your enterprise apart from competitors and soon reap the benefits. It's not rocket science, you know."

I found myself wondering again whether it could really be that simple. Could a few leaders such as Tom and I and those we trusted most restructure an entire culture by simply being honest, open, and transparent, holding one another and others accountable to the principles we would set in place?

Again it seemed as if the old man was able to read my mind.

"Jack," he said, "there is something very powerful about everyone in an organization consistently demonstrating accountability. I mean, think about it for a second. If accountability is in place, you no longer need to look over your shoulder all the time as you most likely have been doing. You would waste less time and energy; production would increase; and everyone would benefit."

"It just can't be that easy."

"I never said that it would be *easy*," he quickly retorted. "Good things, let alone great things, don't come easy. And, of course, you can't create such a culture overnight. But if you don't begin somewhere, not only are you taking a risk, but the longer you wait to change course the harder it will become to do so. It sounds as though you have a great starting foundation in yourself and Tom. In many ways a solid, two-way friendship between business partners is the perfect platform for launching such an ambitious endeavor as company-wide accountability. And that's doubly important when it comes to the vice of greed."

"Why so?"

"Because, as determined as we might be to do the right things, greed has a way of sneaking up on us at any time. It takes accountability within a core group of people to maintain the new structure once you've created it. And that kind of foundational accountability is actually satisfying. There is a sense of being galvanized around an ethical good and being rewarded as a result. You know, that whole 'band of brothers' deal."

I thought about Tom. I was incredibly lucky, or blessed you might say, to have a partner such as Tom. No matter what was going on, I always knew that there was at least one person other than Katherine, of course, to whom I could go to in complete trust and confidentiality.

"And what about you?" I asked. "With whom do you maintain accountability?"

"Oh," he said, leaning back in his chair and looking up at the night sky. Clearly my question had surprised him and struck some sentimental chord. "I am incredibly fortunate to have a few Toms in my life, some lifelong friends who never let much time pass before checking up on me. They ask me hard questions. They don't accept pat answers. They know me well enough to know if I'm not divulging the entire truth. They also care enough about me to let me keep some things close to the chest if I so choose. And I practice the same with them. I'm pretty blessed myself, you might say."

"Sounds like it," I said, feeling an extra measure of gratitude for both Tom and Katherine.

Conversation stalled, and the old man looked down into his wine glass. It was empty.

"Listen," he said, "I'm planning to go fishing in the morning. Why don't you come over early and join me?"

It sounded like a splendid idea. I loved to fish. It was something I had done regularly with my father while growing up but rarely found time for anymore.

"I'd love to," I replied. "What time should I be there?"

"Anytime before noon, but the earlier the better. I'll meet you out on the water. If the sun is already high, look for me in the shaded areas close to shore just north of the path. If the skies are cloudy, you'll find me out in deeper water where the big fish are."

"Sounds fantastic. Should I bring anything? I have no equipment with me, of course."

"I've got you covered. There are plenty of rods and reels lying around the cottage."

He put down his wine glass and stood to leave. I followed suit.

"But," I said. "how are you getting back to your island? It's dark. Where is your boat? Are you sure you don't want to stay here and spend the night? I'm sure that Katherine wouldn't mind."

"Oh gosh, no, but thank you anyway. I had a fine time tonight, Jack. Good conversation and an absolute joy to meet your amazing Katherine."

I nodded in agreement. "Thanks for making the effort to come here. I hope that it's not the only time you two are together."

Now it was he who nodded. Then without delay he started down toward the shore. A few clouds had moved over the moon and hidden the stars above, so that I could barely make out the waterline. I was trying to see what kind of boat might be moored down there, curious about the old man's means of inter-island transportation, but before I could make out any vessel he began to fade into the hazy darkness.

I turned away and then suddenly whirled back around. "Wait!" I shouted into the darkness. "How will I find you if the sun is high and you're tucked back into one of those lagoons?"

From out of the darkness I could hear his voice carried back to me on the ocean breeze. "Come on, Jack. Don't you trust by now that you will find your way?"

His voice faded, his figure completely absorbed by the shadows, and I never did see how he departed from the island. His final words segued into the gentle lapping of surf against shore. I turned and began to walk back toward the bungalow.

9

On the Water

"Come on, boy," the soldier said. "The sooner this is over the better for both of us. You get more oats, and I can get back to this God-awful war."

The horse brayed and looked away, but he allowed the man to approach and did not bolt when he reached out to reclaim the reins. It was as if he understood and was considering some kind of mutual compromise. The soldier clutched the reins a bit more tightly this time and once again began to lead the stallion around the corral. The great horse continued to toss his head as if agitated, but he did not break his cadence and completed a full circle at the man's leading.

"Good boy, good boy," the man said. "That's the way."

They made another round and still another before the man tried something different. He changed course and reversed direction, then led the horse directly across the clearing, making sure that the great stallion was willing to go against a pattern and respond to guidance instead of learned routine. This was repeated several times, and then the man stood at the horse's side and calmly stroked that long-boned cheek. This time, with only a slight lifting and lowering of his head, the stallion allowed the affection.

As soon as I awoke the next morning, I knew immediately that I had enjoyed a little too much wine the night before. Instead of getting up at my normal vacation hour, I slept well past the initial climbing of the tropical sun. Once awake, I bounded from the bed and rushed into the living area to grab some coffee and ask for Katherine's blessing on yet another selfish solo outing. Apparently the old man's charm had granted me an unexpected leverage. Katherine thought that I might benefit from some more time in his presence and eagerly, even hurriedly, helped me to pack the necessities and ushered me out the door. I was careful to tuck my list of vices into the deepest pocket of my cargo shorts.

The kayak-rental manager was awaiting my arrival, now used to my daily tourist routine. There was little banter or instruction any more. A few head nods, my acknowledgment of the rules, a couple of signatures, and I was off. Not thirty minutes after awaking, I was lying back in the kayak, eyes closed, and about even with the floating marker, waiting on a magical storm as my portal to the old man's hidden island. But the storm didn't come. I waited, checked my watch, studied the skies, and forced my eyes closed again and again, believing that was a necessary part of the ritual. Still, no storm. What was going on? Was I somehow being penalized for not awaking earlier?

The sky was empty of clouds, and soon the sun was directly overhead. I grew more frustrated at each passing moment. The old man had instructed me to arrive before noon, and now I was pushing that limit. I suddenly felt like a college freshman who had overslept and was in danger of missing an important class. The minutes passed, and my body was withering away in the noonday sun. Pretty soon my anxiety was replaced by anger, and I shouted up into the heavens. My hands collapsed against my face, trying to block out the burning sun. I had applied a liberal coating of sunscreen, but it was vanishing with my profuse sweat and now burned my eyes. My hands moved down to my neck, and suddenly I sat upright in the kayak.

The shell necklace was gone! Every other time a storm arose and I passed through to the other side, the necklace had been with me.

As quickly as I could, I turned the kayak around, paddled furiously, and made landfall in less than five minutes. I pulled the boat up onto the sand, flipped it over, sprinted to tell the rental manager that I'd forgotten something in my room, and then ran as fast as I could to the bungalow.

As I burst through the door of our cottage, I startled Katherine. She was out on the back porch reading and jumped to her feet when she heard me enter. I shouted that I had forgotten something. I didn't want to say what because that would necessitate an explanation as to why the necklace was so important. I would just be a minute, I told her with apologies for interrupting her reading, and disappeared into the bedroom. I flung the sheets off the bed, fumbled around with the pillows. There, half buried under the headboard, I found my necklace. The loop had broken, but there was enough cord to tie a crude knot. Donning the necklace, I rushed back out of the cottage. "Found what I was looking for," I shouted over my shoulder to Katherine. "See you in a few hours. Love you, honey!"

In fifteen minutes I was back on the water in my previous position. I made sure that the necklace was front and center against my chest, as if the heavens above had to see it in all its glory in order to trigger the thundering portal. I closed my eyes.

It worked like magic. Within minutes the clouds gathered, the skies darkened, the rain and wind came, and my kayak began to toss on the ocean's surface. I kept my eyes closed and hung on tight, balancing myself in the boat's cockpit by holding the paddle perpendicular to the gunwales. Soon the storm abated, and I found myself floating on a calm surface not far from the shore of the old man's hidden island.

I scanned the horizon in all directions, searching for the old man. The storm had subsided, but the clouds overhead were still thick. I then remembered the old man's words, *"If the sun is already high, look for me in the shaded areas close to shore just north of the path. If the skies are cloudy, you'll find me out in deeper water where the big fish are."* Taking into account the lack of full sun, I ignored the shoreline and studied instead the open ocean. At first I saw nothing, the vastness of the sea and the undulation of its surface obscuring any objects in the distance, but then I saw something gently lifting and falling with the waves' rhythm. I paddled in that direction, and after a few minutes it was clear that there was a small skiff adrift on the ocean. When someone stood and waved in my direction, I waved back and paddled harder.

When I reached his boat, the old man was ready with some ropes. "Here," he said. "Tie these to your bow and stern and then climb aboard."

I did as he said and in another minute or two was sitting on one of the seats in his skiff. The old man handed me a bottle of drinking water, and I took a long, deep gulp.

"Thanks," I said. "Sorry I'm late. No great excuse. It was the wine, I guess, and someone who kept me up late talking."

He smiled.

I started to ask how the fishing was going when suddenly one of two poles in the boat's stern holders began to jerk downward. "Looks like you've got something," I said.

The old man lifted the rod out of its berth and pumped hard twice, the tip curving sharply over. "It's been like this all day," he said. "The overcast skies always bring up the fish, and today has been no exception. Take a look inside that live well." He nodded toward the center of the boat. "And those are just the ones I kept, I returned a dozen smaller ones back to the sea."

I lifted up a latch in the seat, and underneath was a square tank filled with seawater. Inside it half a dozen beefy fish swam in tight circles.

"What kind are they?" I asked.

"Same as this one," he said, hauling in another over the boat's gunwale. "Caribbean sea bass. Delicious. I'm going to make you a late lunch that will have you forgetting about sailboat eggs."

He eased what appeared to be about a five-pound fish over to where I sat, and I gently removed the hook and lowered the sea bass into the livewell where he joined his friends.

"There's another pole in the stern," the old man said. "It's all rigged up for you. You'll find bait in that cooler under the rear seat and a holder over there."

In a few minutes my line was out and my bait suspended in the depths below. I waited. The old man caught another, releasing it back into the water because it was a good bit smaller than the others. Still I waited while he caught another. This one made the cut, and he placed it in the live well with the others.

"Guess I'm not holding my own," I said.

"Try the other side of the boat," the old man said. "I've had much better luck over there."

"But we're out in the middle of the ocean," I replied. "That side looks the same as this one. Same depth too, I imagine. So what's the difference?"

He smiled. "The difference is whether or not you want to catch fish."

Just then he hooked another fish. That was enough for me. I reeled in, checked my bait, and cast across the boat to the other side. When my bait reached the strike zone, a hefty fish immediately hit it.

"Lean back!" shouted the old man. "Don't give the fish leverage."

"Easier said than done," I shouted back. "Something tells me that this is no sea bass!"

Just then the line screamed off my reel as the fish tore into deeper water. I did as the old man had advised and leaned back. Eventually the fish slowed, and I could feel him turn back toward our boat. He fought me now in spurts. The fish would run; I'd pull back; and there would be a moment of stalemate. After I gained a few feet on him, the cycle would repeat itself. It went on like this for a good twenty or thirty minutes. Finally the fish seemed defeated. I lifted the rod's last few feet of line out of the water as the mystery fish surfaced.

The first thing that struck me was its variegated, iridescent colors. The fish was long, pushing three feet I guessed, and stout, a good fifteen inches around its girth, but the brilliant colors captured my attention before anything else. As it broke the top of the water, the head and back showed almost fluorescent greens, yellows, and a touch of pink beneath a magnificent body-length fin of midnight blue. Its blunt head was flushed with the same array of colors, and its forked tail was speckled with orange.

"Mahi-mahi," the old man said. "Our lunch just got an upgrade."

"It's beautiful," I said, a bit breathless. "I've never seen so many colors."

"They actually change color when out of water. In Mexico they are called dorado, but I prefer mahi-mahi. It's an Hawaiian word that means "very strong."

"I can sure see why," I said. "That fish wore me out. My heart is beating like a racehorse's."

Together we took the fish off the hook and lowered it gently alongside the sea bass in the live well. There was barely enough room for the larger fish, and its tail wrapped halfway around the tank.

"I'd say that's enough for today," declared the old man, laying down his rod. "One never wants to get greedy on the ocean. Bad karma for the next outing."

Even though I had landed only one fish, I agreed with him, tuckered out as I was from the unexpected fight.

"Before you get too comfortable, how about reaching into that cooler and grabbing us a couple of beers?" he said, motioning toward the small icebox in the stern.

Soon we were both kicked back in our respective corners, sipping Coronas and swaying on the water's surface with the two boats lashed together.

"Did you remember to bring your list?" the old man said after a few moments.

"Got it right here," I said, reaching deep into the pocket of my shorts and producing it. My eyes worked their way down the list until I reached the fifth entry. "This is a bit ironic," I said.

"How so?"

"Well," lifting my eyes to the tranquility surrounding me, "because at this moment the vice seems a world away."

"This might be the perfect state of mind in which to discuss it, whatever it is. Usually, when we are a bit removed from the reality of something, we have a better perspective from which to evaluate it."

I nodded and looked back at my list.

"Well?" said the old man. "Are you going to tease me?"

"Anger," I said.

"*Anger*?" replied the old man, sounding a bit disappointed.

"What's wrong?" I countered. "You don't think that anger belongs on my list?"

"No, that's not it. On the contrary, I'm intrigued. I've very interested to hear how you came up with that as a vice."

I stuffed the list back in my pocket and took another sip of cold beer.

"I don't know. It's just that I sense so much anger around me on a daily basis. Others might not call it by that name, but when I sift through a lot of the junk that oozes out of people and into their business dealings, I think that it's rooted in anger. I can't say exactly why or where it comes from."

«I don't disagree with you at all," the old man interjected. "In fact, I think you are on to something profound, but let me ask you this. Have you ever seen anger as a positive emotion?"

I took my time before responding. Suddenly I knew the perfect example. "Well, yes," I said. "In athletics."

"How so?"

"I've been on teams and watched athletes who are able to control their anger and unleash it at an opportune time as motivation, using it to overwhelm opponents and win competitions. I guess you could say that's a positive use of anger."

"Great example," said the old man. "And the key is the verb you used for managing anger."

"'Control'?"

"Bingo.. First of all, I think it's important to realize that anger comes in different varieties. Not all anger is created equal, you could say."

He sat up now and put his Corona in a drink holder fastened to one of the boat's gunwales.

"There is *selfish anger*," the old man proposed. "There is *righteous anger*, *anger over injustice*, and *repressed anger* that comes out as bitterness. Lovers are moved by *protective anger* to safeguard the one they care most about. But when anger is *controlled*, it can be an incredibly powerful tool.

Used to advance a worthy cause and not in a way that harms another, anger is highly motivational."

"You almost make anger sound like a noble character trait," I said, with a half chuckle.

"I don't know whether I would go that far, but it isn't always the evil beast that some make it out to be."

"It does seem as though you are challenging my latest selection for the list."

"No," he said, "I'm truly not. Sadly it belongs there as much as, if not more than, the others."

"What makes you say that?"

"Because an overwhelming number of people don't leverage and control anger in the way I just described. Instead they let anger control *them*. And uncontrolled anger can be the beast of all beasts. That kind of anger is destructive and wreaks havoc everywhere it's unleashed."

I nodded. "That sounds like the anger I've encountered in the business world." I looked away, my mind suddenly littered with countless examples of how a person's anger had derailed a business venture, sinking a once promising endeavor and harming others along the way. My eyes gazed on the horizon as I silently confessed that I too had allowed uncontrolled anger to get the best of me.

The old man seemed to sense my personal chagrin and didn't want me to linger there too long.

"The problem with anger is that it doesn't stop there," he said. "If it goes unchecked and remains uncontrolled, anger almost always leads to bitterness, especially where relationships are involved."

"People get hurt," I said almost unconsciously, my mind tracking right along with the old man's.

"People get hurt," he affirmed. "That's correct, but maybe even worse than just hurt. Anger and bitterness can easily leave a person feeling judged, rejected, inadequate, and, in a worst-case scenario, pushed beyond restoration. We often say, 'Why can't they just get over it? Buck up. Show some backbone.' But we know it isn't always that easy. What if some people can't just 'buck up'? What if, while they may seem to show strength on the out-side, they are irreparably damaged on the inside? That isn't going to bode well for a company trying to pull together and realize greater corporate success."

He was touching a lot of nerves in me. I'd seen that kind of rejection time and time again in the professional world. I'd even felt such judgment and rejection as a young businessman. In fact, I'd inflicted some myself as a supervisor in my middle age, no doubt thinking that was expected and just part of the process.

"There's something else," the old man said.

"It gets worse?"

"It can," he admitted. "What most people don't acknowledge is that the person who really suffers in that scenario is the one acting out in anger toward another."

"I don't follow you."

"It's an old psychological truth that almost always proves itself over time," he explained. "A person's anger morphs into bitterness. Left un-checked, that bitterness roots itself deeply in the soul of the host. The host holds on tight to that bitterness and uses it as leverage over those under his authority. Such people can't seem to let go of the anger and bitterness because they think that doing so will mean forfeiting their position of power and admitting weakness. The person or persons they are acting out against suffer, but the host suffers even more. And in most cases it takes the host longer to recover once the anger is dealt with and released."

The old man finished speaking, and we both returned to sipping our drinks. The clouds had parted, the sun was shining again, and the cold beer felt refreshing. I searched for something positive in our discussion.

"So what can we do about it all?" I asked.

"*Twice richer is the one who pours out compassion on others, for he in turn will receive double the dose of the same.*" Added the old man, "Legacy Virtue number five—acceptance."

I drained the last of my drink and waited for more exposition.

"Once again, it's not rocket science. Simply put, compassion in the form of acceptance is the strongest defense against the vice of anger."

A wind gust lifted the boat a little higher than normal, and I grabbed the sides to steady myself. The old man seemed unfazed and went on speaking.

"The reality is that when you are asking for high accountability from people, as is normally the case with a successful business, there are going to be times when they fail to meet expectations. But people are different. Even when working collaboratively, they are individuals first. And you must deal with them individually, taking their personal cases into consideration. It's like what an old friend of mine used to say: 'Meet them where they're at.'"

"What does that mean?"

"It means that in order to draw the best out of people, you must be willing to accept them, at least initially, where they are at that moment, not where you want or think they ought to be. That's key. It's an act of what I like to call 'social and practical mercy.' It means that you can accept a person without necessarily accepting his behavior or beliefs. One of the keys to the virtue of acceptance is the ability to discern emerging positive traits in a person under your authority and articulating them in a positive way."

"You mean that by accepting people as they are, you are actually more likely to empower them?"

"Exactly," the old man confirmed. "Too many times our natural tendency is to categorize people. If they meet our criteria, we accept them. If they do not, we reject them. Sometimes in business we have to make quick decisions, but if our decisions are based upon a need to protect ourselves, it may lead to the rejection of others. If we only surround ourselves with people who agree with us, we miss out on perspectives that could spell the difference between success and failure. Different perspectives often lead to innovative breakthroughs in business, whereas the angry, bitter, and close-minded approach is very limiting."

He was right. It wasn't so complicated. This dynamic played itself out far too often in both the professional and personal worlds. Even within the sphere of my own family I had been guilty of this.

"It's a foolhardy way to operate," the old man continued, "especially if your vocational goal is increased success, production, and profitability. Instead of wallowing in anger because a partner or a co-worker doesn't quite 'measure up,' by accepting them where they are at a particular moment you are in actuality setting them up for future success. And of course the more they succeed, the more your company succeeds."

"It seems so simple," I said. "I wonder why it's so hard to operate that way on a consistent basis?"

The old man smiled again. "Because of that same old beast we spoke about earlier—human nature."

"Tell me more," I urged.

"We hold onto anger as a protective measure out of fear, a fear of being vulnerable and transparent, because most likely, at some point along the way, we too have been judged and rejected for not meeting someone else's standard. We are just acting the way we've been taught. So there has to be a willingness to shift paradigms. That takes courage and risk, but it all begins with acceptance of others but also of ourselves. And while uncontrolled anger sucks the energy out of a business, acceptance *infuses* it with energy. Acceptance allows personal discovery and innovation to emerge so that people can function at their highest level."

He then paused and locked his eyes on mine. "Jack, *you* have to be the kind of leader who sets the tone, who recognizes the giftedness in people and can articulate it to them in a way that offers a constructive path toward improved performance. And that starts with simple things like affirmation, empowerment, and encouragement. All those things are part of a person's feeling accepted. And acceptance is the first and perhaps most important step in motivating a team. Once your team is headed down that path, you will discover that the virtue of acceptance leads to a culture where there are few hidden agendas or undercurrents. Your co-workers start to trust one another as well as you, and that sets everyone up for greater success."

I found little to argue with in the old man's words, yet one thing left me a bit unsettled. "But if I practice this virtue of acceptance with all those I'm charged with leading, isn't it possible that I will fall into a trap of acquiescence that could cause me to compromise the goals of the company?"

"Absolutely not," he said without hesitation. "It's completely possible to accept a person while disagreeing with him at the same time. In order to gain acceptance, you needn't give in to that which isn't right. You can listen to the other person, assess the validity of what he is saying, and then decide whether or not you should accept or help to correct his position. Even in pointing out deeply held areas of disagreement, it's still good practice for both parties to accept each other as individuals. Much of the time we feel reluctant to offer the olive branch of acceptance for fear that we will appear to be softening our position, but that doesn't have to be the case at all."

"How does one avoid that scenario?"

"Great question," the old man said. "I'm glad that you asked it. The answer is by being known. A strong, confident leader can be transparent about his own failures and readily admit to them. Let's be honest: it's easy to see the guilt in others who have offended us, but it's much harder to admit our own guilt in a matter. However, when we are courageous in our willingness to acknowledge personal responsibility, make restitution, and ask for forgiveness, we affect others around us positively. But in order to run a team that way, you must attempt to understand a person first before you try to get him to understand or adopt your position. In any organization characterized by high accountability, it should be communicated that rejection of particular courses of action is not rejection of the person."

The old man seemed to sense that my mind was becoming overloaded. "It's a lot to digest, I know," he said. "On the surface the concept of acceptance seems so simple, but much lies beneath it."

"Kind of like an ocean," I said, taking advantage of the most immediate metaphor available.

"Just like an ocean," he agreed and looked down. "Speaking of the ocean, I just thought about what she gave us today." He looked toward the live well that held the fish. "If we're going to enjoy this treasure we've been blessed with, we need to get these guys gutted, cleaned, and laid on ice pretty soon. There doesn't seem to be much of a current. If we're lucky, we can be back at the cottage in less than an hour and eating grilled mahi-mahi not long after that."

I suddenly realized that I was incredibly hungry. I nodded in agreement.

The old man steadied his skiff so that I could climb into the kayak. I untethered my boat from his and pushed away a few feet.

"Follow me," he said, and together we made for the shore.

10

The Stones

The routine was repeated over the next two days, and then the horse sensed a change. To begin with, there was the bulky leather saddle that the soldier was carrying. Until now the stallion had been used only as a pack-horse loaded down with provisions weighing nearly three hundred pounds. He had never been ridden, but he recognized the tack in the man's hands and bristled while being led into the makeshift corral. After two complete passes around it, the soldier looped the reins around a rail and hauled the saddle up and over the stallion's broad flanks. The beast bellowed and shifted and studied the movements of the man out of one eye.

"Easy boy," said the soldier. "It's a big day for you and me. Let's work together on this."

Then the man climbed a few rails beside the horse and eased one leg down and over its wide back. Immediately the stallion bucked, and the man withdrew his leg.

"Now come on, boy," he said, more sternly this time. "It has to happen either this day or the next." He reached down and patted the stallion's tensed neck. "You know me now, boy. We're no longer strangers."

Again the soldier eased one leg down and then the other, still clutching the top of the rail post for balance. "That's it boy," the man said softly.

Slowly, with caution but purpose, the rider let go of the post, gathered up the reins, and then in a fluid movement the two of them moved off, following that same circular pattern as before but now as one graceful entity. Anyone watching from a distance would not have imagined that it had been less than a week since their first encounter.

I beached my kayak near the mouth of the now familiar path. Then I waded back out into the surf and carefully climbed into the old man's skiff just beyond the low breakers. He guided the boat parallel to the shore for a good half mile and then eased it into the mouth of a narrow lagoon. We tied up at a small dock that the old man told me he had built many months earlier.

"When I sense a storm of any size coming," he said, "I rush out here and remove the motor, flip the skiff over, and lash it down extra tight." He looked up at the sky. "I think she'll be alright tonight. There doesn't seem to be any sign of bad weather."

He produced a couple of fillet knives, and together we made quick work of cleaning the fish. We tossed the stripped carcasses into the lagoon, and immediately a flock of birds dove down on them, carting off what they could and leaving the rest for crabs and scavenger fish.

The old man lay the fillets neatly into a large wicker creel that he had left on the dock that morning. The mahi-mahi slabs dwarfed the sea bass, and he remarked again on what a special catch mine was.

The walk to the cottage was much shorter than I imagined, perhaps half the distance of the forest tunnel. Within a few minutes we were inside the cozy bungalow. The old man wasted no time in preparing the meat. While I went out back at his instruction and readied his small charcoal grill, he wrapped the sea bass and placed them in the freezer before lathering the thick fillets of mahi-mahi in a lemon-herb marinade. He then oven-toasted some French baguettes while the grill was heating up, brought the fillets outside, and turned them over to me.

"That's a lot of pressure," I said. I had never been known for my grilling skills. I was a little anxious that I might mess up this tasty fish.

The old man smiled and patted me on the shoulder. "I have a feeling that you can pull it off. Besides, some say it's all about the marinade anyway."

I went about grilling the fish with as much concentration as I could muster. When the portions were done, I asked for his inspection, and he gave me a thumbs-up. He carried the finished product back inside and then reappeared a few minutes later carrying a tray with two generous fillets spilling out from inside the toasted baguettes, complete with lettuce, tomato, and a sprinkling of lemon pepper. He carried a few soft drinks in his other hand. Soon we were seated in the shade and engaged in savoring every bite of the freshly caught fish.

There was little talk between us as we concentrated on the meal, but once our plates were empty we both leaned back and sighed. Suddenly I was overcome with a strange intuition. It came to me so strongly that I had to say something.

"I don't know why," I began, "but I have an overwhelming feeling that I'm not going to be with you much longer, that my time visiting your island is coming to an end."

The old man sipped his drink and seemed to consider my words before speaking. "Perhaps," he said, "but right now the taste of that mahi-mahi is still lingering on my palate, and I'm choosing just to enjoy the pleasure of your company."

A few minutes passed before I was hit again by the same sensation. I couldn't keep it at bay, and my mind returned to the list we had yet to finish. If our time together was drawing to a close, I wanted to benefit from as much of the old man's wisdom as possible.

"Do you mind if I pick up where we left off out on the water?" I asked somewhat sheepishly, not wanting to ruin his after-meal state of mind.

"Not at all," he replied. "Do you have more thoughts on anger and acceptance?"

"Actually I was hoping that we could tackle the next vice on my list."

"Splendid idea," the old man answered.

I produced the folded list from my pocket and laid it out on my legs, staring at the word that followed *anger* on the page.

"What's the matter?" the old man said.

"This one is a bit of an embarrassment. Of course it's on here because I'm guilty of practicing it. And, well, it's pretty damning."

"You can't cure diseases without embracing their diagnosis first," the old man said. "But I know that I'm telling you what you already realize."

I nodded in agreement. "Okay, then, here goes. *Dishonesty.*"

He collected his thoughts for a moment. "Hmm, yes. I can see why you might find that one embarrassing, but it's a universal condition prompting guilt and shame. To use a metaphor that's fitting for today, we're all in the same boat. Although some would deny it, we all stand accused. And we've been guilty of dishonesty since not long after birth."

"What do you mean?"

"Shortly after we come into this world the not so glorious effects of human nature kick in, and we start behaving accordingly. Ironically, it often starts with our parents and, even more surprising, is a direct result of love."

I studied the old man's face, somewhat disappointed in myself. We had been together now for the better part of three days and spent hours upon hours working through my list, yet I was drawing a blank in trying to understand him now.

"Okay, I am thoroughly lost and confused."

He laughed. "It's what I call the Center of the Universe Syndrome. Think about it. From the moment most of us are born, there are people who instantly love us, gathered around, staring down at this new wonder, cooing and sighing and telling us we are the most amazing thing in the world. Seems normal, right? Seems like a good thing?"

I nodded, deeply curious as to where he was going with this line of thought.

"If we as humans could handle those initial months and years of adulation, we'd be okay. The problem is that most of us cannot, and what begins as positive affirmation all too often gives way to narcissism. We enter life being told that we are the center of everyone's world, and before long we truly believe that we are the center of *the* world."

I was skeptical. "But that doesn't make us all bad people," I said. "Surely you can't pin the blame for all of the world's social ills on the well-meaning, even natural love of parents and family for a child?"

"No, not at all," my interlocutor said. "That would be too simplistic. The problem comes later when that initial love and affirmation segue way into the self-promoting culture that pervades most of the civilized world. It isn't that the ones who truly love us unconditionally keep working to make us feel special and important. Of course that is needed for a healthy sense of identity. The problem comes when we realize that the world at large doesn't really care about us as individuals. Hence arises the 'me-first' culture that has spread from the Western world to the ends of the earth. It's the instant-gratification, must-have-it-now-and-step-on-others-to-get-it mentality that is so prevalent in today's world. That's the problem. That's where things go south."

"Leading us to behave in ways that might not be appropriate," I volunteered, "ways counterproductive to a healthy society." Then I made the leap to which I thought he was leading me. "Even the willingness to be dishonest."

"Sadly, yes," the old man said. "You see, dishonesty perpetuates itself because the world somehow convinces us that it's justified. We learn this at an early age, and then the belief gains momentum as we get older. We call others out on it but don't recognize the same behavior in ourselves. In some ways it's nothing more than years of practiced denial. We find justification for any action, no matter how dishonest it might be."

"From the playground to the boardroom," I said, my gaze lazily wandering to the tops of the trees that stood at the edge of the island forest.

"What do you mean?" asked the old man.

"It's just as you said," I replied, without taking my eyes off the treetops. "It's been with me my whole life—the willingness to distort the truth in the most innocent of environments to the workplace. The scary part is how much more prone to dishonesty we seem to become as we get older."

The old man was silent, tacitly inviting me to dig deeper.

"In many ways it's as simple as the old 'He or she did it' line of defense. As juvenile as that sounds, I see it practiced in word and deed all too often. A person blames someone else's willingness to be untruthful as justification for his own dishonesty. Again it's an almost childish reversion to the thinking that two wrongs make a right."

"Are you connecting some dots?" the old man asked.

"I think so. It's narcissism run amok, I guess, going all the way back to birth. It's almost as though the umbilical chord of self-promotion was never cut."

"Ha! I don't think I ever entertained that particular image, but I like it. It fits."

"It really does," I said, pleased with my comparison. "If in fact we have been conditioned to believe that we are the center of the universe since birth, then it only follows that as we grow older we might be willing to justify our dishonesty on the grounds of our special standing in the world, even if that world is limited to our own individual soul."

"I think you're right on the money," the old man chimed in, "but there is another and perhaps equally motivating factor at work."

"What's that?"

"A kind of self-preservation. People justify their dishonesty because they begin to think it's their best, maybe their only, recourse. They are afraid to face certain circumstances that come along with being honest. As people grow older and somewhat cynical about the world they live in, perhaps with good reason, the seeds of distrust are sown, and any faith they had in their fellow man is shattered. They fall into the trap of believing that if they're always transparent things won't work out and the world will turn against them."

To his line of explanation I added, "'Honesty is the best policy' gets tossed out the window."

"And trampled underfoot until it's unrecognizable."

I looked at him and shook my head, signaling a loss as to what he meant by those last words.

"Sometimes deceitfulness is glaring and obvious," he said, "but as people grow older and learn the artful tricks of deception, it can become subtle, hidden, almost unnoticeable at times. I imagine that in your business circles this is much more the case."

I now, understood exactly what he meant. I had detected the subtleties of deception in the workplace time and time again, and I was not exempt from them. If I took the time to think it through, I imagine that I would be disgusted with my own willingness, however programmed and seemingly unintentional, to engage in such unethical behavior.

The sun had dipped close to the edge of the tree line, and I repositioned my chair to shield my eyes from its glare. Then I shifted the conversation to what I hoped would be a more uplifting topic.

"So," I said, "what's the escape from such cyclical madness?"

The old man gathered his thoughts before replying, "*The one who sets himself apart, protecting the honor of his core, will gain an audience with the source of all that is good and right.*" Immediately sensing my befuddlement, he added: "I know. It does sound a bit overwhelming and weighty."

"Yet another understatement," I said.

"*Integrity*, Jack. It's all about integrity."

"The sixth virtue?"

"Exactly."

"Those are pretty loaded words," I commented. "Honor and integrity—it sounds as though you're setting an especially high bar."

"That's true," the old man agreed, "but it has to be, because the world has lowered the bar so greatly. Only a dramatic swing in the right direction has a chance to change things."

Of course I knew that the old man was right. "So you're saying that a commitment to integrity has the power to offset the disease of dishonesty," I summarized.

"Well said," the old man replied. "You are becoming quite the accomplished student of the Great 8."

"I have a pretty solid teacher."

We both shifted in our chairs as if preparing for an even higher plane of discussion.

"A person of integrity," the old man began, "acts consistently with everyone with whom he interacts. There is no discrimination. There is only one standard, no matter whether the environment is the workplace or home. A person of integrity, to borrow a courtroom phrase, tells the truth and nothing but the truth."

"That's easier said than done," I offered.

"Yes, no doubt, but, before you dismiss what seems like the unattainable, you have to consider *why* you automatically default to that position."

"And what would that be?"

"Much of what we have already discussed," said the old man. "Insecurity. Fear. The defensive belief that if we are always honest it will cost us something. In a way it's as simple as the principle of delayed gratification. In the short term being dishonest may appear to bring us some benefit. To use an example from the business world, it's incredibly tempting to promise clients something you can't deliver because you are desperate to close a deal."

I nodded knowingly. I had seen this a million times and was guilty of it myself.

"In truth," the old man continued, "when we are honest, even to the sacrifice of an immediate profit, in the long term we and our business will benefit. Honesty and integrity create a reputation of credibility that will provide returns far into the future. Clients learn to depend on your business. They trust that you will actually deliver what you promise. And even more, among your business partners a sense is created that everyone is committed to doing the right thing. Nothing holds a workplace together more than a collective buy-in. Stability is fostered, longevity is established, and ultimately greater productivity and prosperity are the reward."

"It seems so elementary," I remarked. "It's amazing how far we can stray from what we know is right."

"Yes, and it's amazing to me how people and companies are willing to keep living with the consequences of their bad practices. Integrity enables an organization to weather the storms of adversity and protect its brand, whereas dishonesty and compromise create the exact opposite."

"It sounds as though you're saying that dishonesty divides, separates, and alienates, whereas integrity unites, validates, and honors."

"If I didn't know better," said my host, "I'd say you were reading ahead."

I laughed. "Praise gratefully received, but I didn't know there was a book. Is there?"

"There's always a book," he replied. "Not much is original in the present. But there's no substitute for authentic human interaction. If I handed you something to read or, even worse, *emailed* you a document, imagine all the intangibles that would have been lost from the past few days of being together face to face."

"Good point," I said.

"Actually," the old man announced, "I have something even better than a book."

"What's that?"

"A pile of rocks."

I stared at him, looking puzzled. Then he motioned for me to follow him as he walked toward the opening of the path that I had followed the day I discovered him high upon the bluff overlooking the sea. It was growing darker now. The sun had slipped low, but there was still enough light at the edge of the yard to see the beginning of the path. For a moment I thought that he was going to enter it. I instantly recalled his accident the morning we descended down the path, and I raised my hand to stop him, convinced that this was a bad idea in the fading daylight. But then he paused, standing just outside the entrance to the path beside a stack of large round stones. I remembered them now. They had caught my eye the morning I ventured up the path shortly after sunrise. He put his hand on the top stone.

"Eight stones," he said, and I immediately understood the number's significance.

"The Legacy Virtues," I said. "The Great 8."

"Exactly," he confirmed. "Now feel how strong the stones are." He motioned me over to his side.

The eighth stone on the cairn came up to my mid-chest. I reached out and rested my hand on the middle stone.

"Push," he said.

I pushed lightly, but nothing happened.

"Harder," he prompted. I obliged. I felt a little movement, but not much.

"They're pretty heavy," I said.

"Yes," he agreed. "*Together* they are. Together they work to forge a stronger unit."

Then he reached out with both hands, cupping them under the edges of the highest stone and gently lifted it. Bending his knees, he lowered the stone to the ground. Just watching him crouch, I could tell that the top-most stone was heavy. He stood upright again.

"Now," he said. "Try again. Try to push them."

I did as he directed. This time, while still quite heavy, the stones betrayed a slight displacement. It would take a real effort to topple them, but it was clear that without the capstone they were not as difficult to manipulate.

"Try the ones at the bottom," the old man said.

I bent low and pushed against the foundational stone. There was no give whatsoever. I wiped the stony grit off my hands and stood up.

"Do you understand?" he asked.

"Yes," I said. "I think that I do."

"Tell me."

"The virtues work together," I began. "If you remove even one, they remain strong, but not as strong as when they are fully united."

"Bravo, Jack. Go on."

"They sort of feed off each other. In a way I guess that you could say they even need each other."

"Again, very good. And what about the lesson of the lower stones?"

"Well, the upper stones sort of protect the lower ones. Their weight, or perhaps their significance, helps the lower ones to maintain their stability. The cairn's overall strength and stability depend on the total mass. Likewise," I extrapolated, "the virtues, when practiced together, lend each other power if accepted as a collective whole. They can be defined individually, as we have been doing, but their potential efficacy is best realized when they stand together."

"Well done, Jack," the old man said. "*Very* well done."

I nodded and thanked him.

"Now," he said, looking down, "do an old codger a favor and spare me the task of replacing the stone I removed."

"Of course," I said. I squatted and replaced the stone atop the tower. "Stones seven and eight," I murmured, "the last two virtues."

"Yes?"

"I can't wait to find out what they are."

"In time," the old man said, "in due time."

Time. As soon as he said the word, I was struck by a deep conviction that I was in fact *out of time*. As much as I had enjoyed the old man's company and treasured our discussions, I knew that I needed to leave immediately. A heavy sense of dread, almost gloom, washed over me. The old man must have sensed the dramatic change in my demeanor, for he reached out his hand and placed it on my shoulder.

"What is it, Jack? You look las though you just saw a ghost."

"I don't know," I replied, "but something is terribly wrong."

I immediately thought of Katherine, and as the moments passed I became more and more convinced that something had happened to her.

"I have to go," I said. "I'm sorry. I'm really sorry. Today has been great—the fishing. the lunch, our conversation. But I have to go and find out what's happening. I've never felt like this before. I don't claim to be psychic in any sense of the word, but somehow I know there's something bad wrong, and I need to find out what."

"Of course," the old man said. "Stop apologizing and go."

And so I did. I hastily waved goodbye and walked quickly to the edge of the woods on the far side of the property. Once there, I entered the forest and broke into a jog. The jog became a run, and by the time I reached the beach I was in an all-out sprint. I rushed the kayak into the water and paddled hard into deep water. It never occurred to me to look back at the island. Perhaps I would have, had I known that it would be the last time I ever visited there, but my focus was solely on the watery horizon in front of me and, beyond it, my precious Katherine. I prayed to the heavens above, "Please let Katherine be okay."

The distance between the island and my kayak quickly increased until the island disappeared altogether. At the time I could not have known that I would never again stand on its shores and never again visit the old man in his cottage tucked away in the jungle. I didn't know it then, but in time the island would come to haunt me in a deep, ever-present way. But for now all of that was lost on me. My entire world, indeed my very existence, had been reduced to putting every ounce of energy I could muster into paddling out to sea.

11

Tom

The sun rose and set, the moon lit the night half a dozen times, and by the end of each day the great horse and the soldier-rider had performed their dance in the dusty clearing at the edge of camp. There was little drama anymore in their daily interaction, but that was a thing to be hoped for—a good omen for those times of chaos and carnage when what was needed was discernment by the one and obedience by the other.

The horse noticed a level of anxiety in the camp that had been absent before. The long shadow of war brought with it an ever-present element of tension, but now it was clear that the shadow was shortening.

Despite the gathering clouds, the stallion and the soldier carried on with their methodical routine. Almost no words were needed anymore. The horse knew the time when the man would appear at his stall. Likewise, the man knew every stride the horse would take as they covered the corral's perimeter. The slightest pressure on the reins prompted the stallion to respond accordingly. Only one word now summed up their mutual bond—trust.

I reached shore and, in my rush to get to Katherine, managed to leave the kayak still in the water. Apparently it drifted back out to sea, never to be found again by the resort staff, resulting in a hefty replacement fee on my next credit-card statement. At the time I could not have cared less. I had to find Katherine. She was not on the beach or in the cottage. I frantically called the reception desk, and in a matter of minutes a mad search was underway for my beloved wife. I got a call back that she had been located sitting by herself and calmly eating lunch in one of the resort's restaurants. I rushed out of the cottage and intercepted her as she was being escorted across the grounds by one of the staff. She looked a bit stunned as I wrapped my arms around her and then pulled back, looking into her eyes.

"You seem fine," I said, clearly surprised.

"Jack, what's the matter with you? I'm fine. I came in from the beach and was having a light lunch."

"Oh," I said, thanking her escort and apologizing for the slight uproar I had caused. After he was out of earshot, I turned back to face her. "I was out, you know, doing my thing, and suddenly I felt that something was terribly wrong. I had this overwhelming sense of panic. I was worried sick about you. You can't know how relieved I am to see that you're okay. I'm so thankful I was wrong."

She looked up at me and sighed, dropping her shoulders.

"What is it?" I said, understanding immediately that she had something to tell me.

"Well, you were partly correct."

"I knew it!" I said. "I knew that something was wrong."

"Yes," she said, "but not with me."

"What then?" I asked, now suddenly panicked about the welfare of our kids and grandkids. "Who?"

"It's Tom," she said. "Beth called the resort and left a message. I called her back while you were gone, and we spoke for a few minutes. He's not doing well at all. The doctors discovered some new lesions yesterday. This morning he asked for you, and Beth relayed the message."

Beth was Tom's wife. I had left the number of the resort with Beth in case of an emergency. Tom had seemed in high spirits when we left for the Caribbean. His doctors all agreed that the chemo was working Tom was even coming into the office twice a week to confer with me on all major deals.

"What did he say exactly?" I asked Katherine.

"He said that he needed to see you. He told Beth that he wanted to reach you a few days ago, but he didn't want to spoil our time away. Then his condition worsened, and he had no choice."

"*Tom*," I whispered, pulling Katherine close to my chest.

"We need to leave, Jack," she whispered into my ear. "He needs you. They need us."

I nodded in agreement.

"I've already spoken to the resort staff," Katherine said. "We can leave the island this afternoon for Miami and catch a flight that gets us into Atlanta before daybreak. We can go straight to the hospital. Beth said that she will meet us there."

"Let's go pack," I said, and arm in arm we made our way back to the cottage.

———————

In a little over an hour our bags were stowed in a floatplane, and we were in our seats ready for take-off. As the aircraft's door was about to close, the same cheery man who had greeted us upon our arrival days earlier reappeared.

"I just wanted to say goodbye," he said, "and to give you something." He reached into his pocket and fished out my shell necklace. "You must have dropped this in your hurry to leave," he said. "The cleaning staff found it and rushed it out to me."

"Thank you," I said, reaching out my hand. I closed my fist around the shell, but when I pulled my hand back, he grasped it and wouldn't let go.

He leaned inside the plane and said, "Your time on the island has come to an end, Mr. Jack, but the things you experienced here will remain with you long after this place is just a memory. Don't forget what you learned here. Let it be forever a part of your life, your soul, and your spirit."

The moment was morphing into something a bit creepy, and I wanted him to let go of my hand.

"Most of all," the man said, now leaning even further into the cabin and dropping his voice to a whisper so that only I could hear, "don't forget the things *he* told you. That was your treasure."

And with that he smiled, let go of my hand, and abruptly shut and latched the cabin door. The next moment we were taxiing down the runway and lifting off into the air. As the plane climbed, the cheery man's words echoed in my mind. Was he talking about the old man? Who else could he have meant? And, if so, how did he know?

As our plane climbed higher, I noticed that the man remained on the dock below, waving the entire time. Finally we passed through a set of low clouds, and that side of the island lapsed from sight. Then we banked to the right in the direction of the beach where I had launched the kayak each day. Suddenly I realized that the flight path was going to take us directly over the old man's island. I stared out the window, hoping to catch a glimpse of the beach, perhaps even of his octagonal cottage, but the island never came into view. Where it should have been was nothing but endless, blue, open water.

"What are you looking for?" Katherine asked, noticing how intently I was studying the ocean's surface.

"Nothing," I said. "Nothing at all."

I slumped down into my seat. Katherine took my right hand in hers. My left held the necklace, my fist still wrapped tightly around it. But there was something different about the necklace, and I quickly realized that it was the weight. The necklace was heavier than before. I unfurled my fist and pried it open. There, ensconced in the open shell, was a beautiful pearl.

12

Atlanta

The storm announced itself soon after nightfall. In the beginning it seemed to come on like any other, but as evening dragged on the winds picked up, the rains strengthened, and by the late hours it was clear that this was like no storm any man in the camp had previously witnessed. It was too late when they began rushing about trying to tie things down. Men abandoned the effort and, fearing for their very lives, hunkered down in whatever shelters remained.

Sometime in the early morning hours, when the storm was peaking, the stables came apart, and the great horse narrowly escaped being crushed by the collapsing trusses of his stable. Instinct told him at the last moment to break clear of the overhead structure. He pulled up twenty yards away from the shattered stables. Half a dozen horses had fled, galloping away into the night. To what future they ran was uncertain. The great stallion resisted the natural urge to follow them, knowing that he was meant for something greater than self-preservation.

Somehow, miraculously, Katherine and I slept on our two flights home. We landed in the pre-dawn hours of an Atlanta morning, made our way through the airport, caught a shuttle to our car, and soon were navigating north to one of the city's largest hospitals. Katherine called Beth, who said that she would meet us at the front desk. Once together, the three of us embraced for what seemed like an eternity.

"Well?" Katherine said, still clutching Beth's hands. "Any changes since we spoke yesterday?"

"No. The doctors say that it could be days or only hours."

"We're here, Beth," Katherine managed to reply. "For you and for Tom. We aren't going anywhere."

Beth found the strength to nod and embrace Katherine again.

"Can we see him?" asked my wife.

Beth wiped her eyes. "Yes, of course. He's been waiting for you. I told him that you were on your way." Then, taking Katherine's hand, she led us toward the elevator and Tom's private room.

"He kept asking me on which day you were returning," Beth said, glancing in my direction. "Tom says that he has something he must tell you, Jack. I would answer him, and then an hour later he would ask again: 'When is Jack coming back? When can I see him? What if he doesn't re-turn before. . . .'"

As we walked the rest of the way, my mind was racing. Thinking about the last few days, I felt as though I had so much to tell Tom, but what in the world did he feel he needed to tell me?

When we entered his private room, Tom was asleep, or so he appeared. I had prepared myself for the worst. Instead, almost shockingly, his face seemed to betray a smile. Beth leaned over the bed and whispered his name. Almost immediately Tom's eyes fluttered open. If he had been asleep, he was floating just beneath the surface of consciousness.

"Sweetheart," Beth said softly. "Katherine and Jack are here. They just landed and came straight to see you."

Tom's eyes opened wider and slowly turned in our direction. "Katherine, Jack," he managed with a strain in his voice. "I'm sorry that you cut your vacation short, but I'm so glad that you're here."

Katherine moved around the side of the bed and found Tom's hand. "We're exactly where we want to be right now," she assured him.

My best friend's smile grew wider, and he found the strength to lift his other hand and lay it over Katherine's. "You have been the best of friends," he said. "both of you. .I can never thank you enough for all the ways you have cared for me and for Beth. Soon," he said, "it's just going to be one of us, but please don't stop caring for my Beth."

Struggling to maintain her composure and on the verge of tears, Katherine nodded. "Of course, Tom," she said. "You know we will, *whenever* that day comes."

Tom craned his neck so that his eyes found mine. I too was holding back my emotions, struggling to play the strong, calm, and collected friend.

"Jack," Tom said, and almost immediately my eyes began to moisten. "I'm here, buddy."

Tom turned back toward Katherine and Beth. "Would you two mind if Jack and I had a few moments?"

"Of course not," Katherine replied. "Anything you want."

"You take all the time you need, honey," Beth said. "We'll be right outside if you need us."

Our wives left the room, and I walked around to Tom's side.

"Why don't you sit down," he said, his voice seeming to strengthen and steady. "I've had too many people hovering over me the last few days." He smiled. "It feels a little intimidating at times."

"Of course," I said, and sitting down in a leather chair near a large picture window that faced the bed.

I had so much I wanted to tell Tom. I wanted to share every detail of the last few days, to tell him all about the hidden island and the old man. I wanted to share my list of vices with him and especially the Legacy Virtues. Instead, I sat frozen, undone by the reality of my best friend lying there in front of me, maybe only days away from leaving this world and passing on to the next. Fortunately, Tom sensed my paralysis and rescued me.

"I know that it's hard to see me like this," he said, "but I want you to know something."

"I'm listening," I replied.

"I'm at peace with everything," Tom said, looking me straight in the eyes. Then his voice quickened a bit, and he spoke with more intent, more purpose. "Maybe for the first time in my life, I'm at peace with myself. I'm at peace with the world. I'm at peace with living, and, well, I'm at peace with dying."

I could only nod. I wasn't sure what he meant, but I found myself nodding anyway.

"That's a great window, isn't it?" Tom said.

I turned to take in the full breadth of the window from where I sat. Again, I wasn't sure what Tom meant, but I nodded anyway.

"It sure is. It's really . . . big," I said, immediately feeling silly for stating the obvious.

"At night, when Beth is asleep in that chair you're sitting in, it feels as though it's just me and that window. It kind of represents the world to me. It's as though I'm staring out the window but not seeing what lies outside. I'm just looking out on a world in which I've become deeply disappointed."

I looked out the window. Sitting in the chair, I was afforded a higher vantage point than Tom. The sun was beginning to rise, and I could see a large park behind the hospital. It clearly had been built just for the hospital. There were benches, walking paths, and a few water fountains. It was a place where patients could visit with family, where family and friends could take breaks from the sometimes depressing and hopeless atmosphere that every hospital can never escape. Beyond lay the tall buildings of Atlanta's downtown skyline, but from where Tom lay I knew that he could see mostly sky and perhaps the tops of a few tall trees.

"The world out there is going to continue," Tom said, "but my life is going to end. At first that realization was horrible to me. I came in here wrestling with all those demons you and I have been dealing with for years: the frustrations over our disappointments at work, the uncertainty of whether or not we might be able to achieve all we set out to accomplish. There were also feelings of inadequacy about how I've been as a husband and as a father. Did I do enough to show Beth and the kids how much I love them? Have I given my kids the necessary tools for successful, fulfilled lives?"

Again I found myself just nodding. Everything he said rang true, and deep down I knew exactly what Tom was talking about. Maybe all men do.

"And then one night I woke up, or rather I felt as though something, or someone, awakened me. There was a soft, gentle voice in the room asking me to open my eyes. At first I imagined it must be Beth, but she was still fast asleep. I looked out that window and saw the most brilliant and magnificent sky I'd ever seen. The stars were more illuminated than I could ever remember. Or maybe I just hadn't paid as much attention to them as I should have in the past. It took my lying here incapacitated in this room to notice them in all their glory. They were beautiful, beyond beautiful really. More like captivating. I couldn't look away."

Tom's words instantly took my mind back to the island. I thought of that first night with the old man when I walked out into the meadow surrounding his cottage and looked up, marveling at the carpet of bright stars over the Caribbean. They were of course the same stars that Tom saw from his hospital bed in suburban Atlanta.

"I was lying here and looking up at that sky," he continued. "It was so magnificent, so majestic. My soul ached to be able to stand and go to the window, then to go beyond the window. I know it sounds silly, but I wanted to pass through that window and float up into the sky and touch those stars. I wanted somehow to connect myself to that beauty, but of course I couldn't do any such thing. In fact, I didn't even have the strength to get up from this bed and walk to the window."

Tom's eyes were fixed on the window, as if he were seeing the scene all over again. I was right there with him but listening to his words in the context of my experience on the old man's island.

"And all of a sudden," Tom said, "I realized that all my life I've wanted to be in control of everything around me. In fact, I thought that I *was* in control most of the time. When things went well, I thought it was because of something I had done. When things didn't go so well, I also imagined that it was a reflection on me and that I was the root cause. I assumed the same attitude in our business life, Jack. Deep down I kept thinking that it was up to us to fix the things that began to trouble us over the last few years. Making things right, I thought, depended completely on me, on us. But lying here, staring out at that magnificent sky and acknowledging that such a scene of perfection existed completely apart from anything I had done, was so utterly freeing. In fact, it made the whole scene even more beautiful because I was just free to enjoy it and marvel at its wonder. I know that must sound corny. Maybe this is what happens when you are close to death, but the feeling of freedom was so strong that I couldn't deny it. And beyond the freedom came a peace I have never before experienced. As I've already said, it was a peace about living, however much longer that may prove to be, and a peace about dying. It's not up to me to make the world a beautiful place. That's going to continue long after I am gone, if only we keep our eyes open and look for it."

I had lost myself in Tom's words. He paused, and the silence momentarily brought me back.

"Are you with me?" he asked.

"Right here, buddy," I said. "Every word. Right here."

"Good," he said. "Just in case you think the medicine they're pumping into me has caused me to wax poetic, I do have a point I'm trying to make. And it has nothing to do with the sky or stars."

"I assure you that you have my full attention."

"Don't own it, Jack," he said. I could tell that Tom was trying to bore the words into my soul.

"*Don't own it*," he said again emphatically. "All the ills of this world, all the things that are not so beautiful, especially in the business world, don't own those things, Jack. It's not our job to make all those things right, to fix all those problems. Don't get me wrong. You need to be the best person you can—the best husband, the best father, the best businessman. You should never stop striving for those goals, but you can't own the fallout from those who aren't willing to live up to that standard. Because what happens is that you start to own that stuff, and then, all of a sudden, you wake up one day and find out that it owns you! That's what happened to you and me, Jack. And when something you can't control owns you, it steals your joy. It steals your very life. You start to defend yourself, and pretty soon you find that you're up against a wall. Jack, we've been living our lives in a defensive mode for too many years now, trying to overcome the dark side of the business world instead of concentrating on creating our own light, even if it's just a little bit of light, because when things get dark even a little bit of light makes a huge difference."

Tom stopped talking then and stared out the window. I detected a look of contentment on his face, which struck me as pretty incredible considering his circumstances. Several moments of silence passed between us. Again I felt a rush come over me, a desire to recount the last few days of my life. I wanted desperately to tell Tom everything that had happened to me. At the same time I had no idea where to start.

"Did you ever study Greek?" I blurted out.

Tom's eyes narrowed, and he looked hard at me. "Excuse me?" he said, probably wondering whether I'd heard a word he'd said.

"In school did you by any chance study Greek?"

He shook his head gently from side to side, staring at me with a quizzical expression. "No. German. And never used it, sad to say."

"Well," I said slowly, "there is a word, *praus*. It's a word the ancient Greeks used to describe a great war horse."

"Go on," Tom remarked, and I proceeded to tell him everything that the old man had taught me about that word, about the war-ready stallion fully committed to his rider in obedience and purpose. I explained how a horse like that knew not to waste its energy on the unimportant and instead be at the ready to unleash the full brunt of his power at the most opportune moment.

Finally, believing that I had represented the essence of the old man's lesson, I said to Tom, "You, my friend, have lived a *praus* life as a husband, as a father, as a businessman, as a friend. You have used your power for good, for the greater good and for the good of those around you. You have been a war horse when your family needed you, when life's circumstances called for it, and. . . ." I paused, my emotions momentarily causing my throat to constrict. "And you were always there for me, Tom. You were a *praus* when *I* needed you to be."

I fell silent then, not sure whether what I was attempting to convey was getting through. A moment passed, and then Tom motioned for me to stand and come closer. I stood over him, and he found the strength to reach up and put his hand on my chest. Again he locked eyes with me.

"Jack, don't give up," he said. "Don't give up, and don't give in. Give things away. Don't let them own you. Love Katherine. Love your kids, and love their kids."

I could only nod, feeling but fighting the seeming finality of his words.

"And if I am the war horse that you spoke of," he added, "if I have lived a *praus* life, then I am passing the torch to you. My race is now your race. You carry the mantle for both of us."

I nodded. What else could I do or say? If I verbally accepted his directive, I felt as though I would be acknowledging once and for all that Tom's life was coming to its end. And I couldn't do that. *I* wasn't ready. Maybe *he* was at peace, maybe *he* was ready to step out into the great unknown of what awaited him on the other side of death, but *I* was not ready for him to go there.

"I think," Tom began to say, his voice sounding weaker, "that I'm going to sleep now. I'm feeling a bit tired."

His grip loosened from mine, and I gently placed his hand back on his chest.

"Of course," I said. "That's a good idea. Rest as much as you need to."

His eyes left mine and began to close before I could say another word. I stood there for a moment watching over him. His chest rose and fell in rhythm as he slept. I studied his face. His expression conveyed the unmistakable presence of an inner peace.

I closed the window shades so that the morning light wouldn't wake him. Then I went to the door, opened it quietly, and peeked outside to see where Katherine and Beth might be. They were nowhere to be seen. Looking once more in Tom's direction, I felt confident that he was okay and resting, so I gently closed the door behind me. As I turned to make my way down the hospital hallway, I had no inkling in my soul that I had just seen my best friend for the last time.

———

Tom died that same day in the middle of the afternoon. Beth was at his side. She said that he was sitting up, holding her hand, and staring out that big window. He seemed perfectly at peace, she told us over the phone shortly after he passed. "Almost content," she said softly, her voice weakened from hours of crying, "as if he were ready for whatever awaited him."

The wake and funeral were set for later in the week. Beth asked me whether I would share a few words, and of course I agreed. In fact I would be honored, I told her. Just before I hung up the phone she added, "Oh, and one more thing, Jack."

"Of course. Anything."

"The last thing he said to me before he drifted asleep for the last time."

"Yes?" I said, a lump rising in my throat as I realized that Beth was sharing one of the most significant moments of her life with me.

"He told me he loved me, of course, and he named each of our kids and grandkids specifically. And then. . . ." She hesitated. "And then he said something I've never heard before. A single word. He kept repeating it over and over again. I leaned in to listen more carefully, but still I didn't recognize what he was saying."

She paused, as if she didn't know how to repeat whatever it was Tom had said.

"What did it sound like?" I asked.

"It was very strange," she said, "almost as if he were saying 'prowess.'"

I smiled to myself and told her I would explain later when we could share a quiet moment in person.

———

The funeral was difficult, as such occasions usually are. It was supposed to be a celebration of Tom's life, at least that's what the program said, but it didn't seem that anyone was celebrating anything. Instead, it was a pretty typical affair, people making nervous small talk as they filed into the church, unsure of what to say at a time like this. When the service began, every pew was filled, and there were even some late arrivals standing in the back. The minister opened the program, a few of Tom's nieces sang a couple of hymns, and then it was my turn. I had prepared some thoughts, even written them down on a card, but as soon as I opened my mouth all the preparation for the moment escaped me. I said something about what a great business partner Tom had been and how my career would have been horribly incomplete without him. I mentioned what a great husband and father he had been, an example for myself and many others. Mostly I talked about the friend he had been to me and how much richer my life was for having known him. And I reminded those in the church of the friend I knew he had been to most of them.

At some point I knew that I was rambling, and then something stopped me cold. As I spoke, my eyes scanned the audience. I was trying to do what all good public speakers are taught to do-—look into the eyes of the audience, find a way to connect with the listeners. As I surveyed the furthest rows, I spotted a familiar face that almost caused me to choke on my words. It was *my* face a quarter century into the future. It was the old man! At first I did a double-take. My speech came to a halt, and I'm sure the audience thought I was choking up with emotion. Then I looked again, squinted, even leaned my head forward. It was he alright. He even smiled at me and lifted his hand slightly to wave. From that moment on I'm not exactly sure what I said. I tried to tie things together with a few short sentences, but they were incomplete and jumbled. Finally, I just tucked my note card back inside my suit jacket and left the stage.

I don't remember the rest of the service. I spent it counting the seconds until the closing hymn and prayer. I waited until Beth and the other members of Tom's family had recessed before making a beeline for the back of the church. The old man was gone, or at least he had already exited from the sanctuary. I found Katherine and told her I had to take care of something. We agreed to meet back at the reception, which was to start in just a few minutes in the church annex on the far side of the property. Then I left through the front door. I searched the parking lot, and when I didn't find him I walked around the side of the main building. There was a city park opposite the church, and I scanned the grounds. I saw him sitting on a park bench, facing away from the church. I couldn't see his face, but I recognized his build, which of course was like my own. I walked briskly in his direction. As I got closer, I could see that he was throwing bread crumbs to a small flock of city pigeons.

"It *is* you!" I exclaimed as I came around and stood in front of him, scaring away the pigeons.

"Yep, it's me," he replied in his typical upbeat, cheery voice.

"But how? I mean, how did you know where to come? How did you get here? When did you leave the island? Speaking of your island, when Katherine and I were leaving I noticed that I couldn't see. . . ."

He cut me off. "Listen, I don't know how long I can stay today. Let's not waste our time with too many unimportant questions."

"Okay," I said. "Just one then."

"Okay," he agreed. "One."

"*Why* did you come?"

"Because," he began, without any hesitation, "I knew that Tom was a great friend to you. I knew that he was extremely significant in your life. I wanted to honor him, to join you in *your* honoring of him. Is that okay?"

I was taken aback for a moment. The gesture on the old man's part was pretty remarkable, considering that he would go to all that trouble and travel that far without ever having known Tom. Now I suddenly felt a tinge of guilt for grilling him about his presence.

"And if all the things that you and others in there said about Tom are true," the old man continued, "I'd say that my being here today was well worth the effort I made to get here."

"Well," I said, "it was incredibly kind of you to come. I only wish you could have known Tom."

"I feel as though I did," the old man said, "through you." He patted the bench beside him. "Now that that's settled, and seeing how you drove my pigeons away, why don't you join me on this lonely bench?"

I sat down beside him. A moment later the pigeons returned, and he began to toss them bread crumbs again. I started to ask him where he got the bread from and then stopped, counseling myself against any more unnecessary inquiries. Instead I described my final moments with Tom. I told him how I had tried my best to explain the meaning of *praus*, how I had suggested that Tom was an exemplar of the concept. Remembering those ideas drew my mind back to the Legacy Virtues and then, a thought later, to my list. My list! In our hurry to depart from the island, I must have left it in the resort's bungalow.

"No, you didn't," the old man said in an uncanny moment of telepathy. Then he reached into the breast pocket of his jacket and pulled out the list. "You left it at my house in your rush to leave the other day." He handed the paper to me.

I looked down at the list, my eyes taking in all the creases, a result of all those kayak trips back and forth to the island. Some of the words were blurry, having been smudged by seawater. When I finally reached the seventh vice, I studied it for a moment and then leaned back on the bench in temporary shock.

"What is it?" the old man said, sensing my discomfort.

"He didn't use this exact word," I said, "but this is precisely what Tom was talking about when I visited his hospital room yesterday. I was overwhelmed by Tom's situation and didn't make the connection at the time." I looked down at the list again. "This is amazing."

"Okay, okay," the old man said somewhat impatiently. "The suspense is killing me. What did you write there?"

"The term I used is *territorialism*." Then I shared how Tom had encouraged me not to "own it," how he had challenged me to let go of the idea that I could somehow fix all the problems around me. "Doesn't that sound eerily familiar?" I asked the old man.

"Well," he said, not as convinced as I was, "it might. Depends on what you meant when you wrote that word on your list. That was a while ago now. Do you remember?"

"In a nutshell," I explained, "I was thinking of the defensive-minded practice that so many in the business world engage in while trying to protect their turf."

"Go on," said the old man.

"I too am guilty as charged," I continued. "You spend so many years on building a client base and a reputation within a company. So it feels normal, even justified, to do anything to protect that construct, even from others *within* your own company."

The old man threw the last of his bread crumbs to the pigeons at his feet. They contorted their necks and, finally convinced that the food source was gone, waddled away.

"Tom and I called this the 'silo effect,'" I said.

The old man shook his head, signaling that he was not familiar with the term.

"Within an organization employees try to pursue cross-selling opportunities with their existing client base. The theory is that a client who has significant needs and resources can be tapped more than once. Maybe my co-worker has opened the door with a particular client but then, for whatever reason, gone no further. I might be the one who can cause the floodgates to open, generating untold revenue down the line for myself and my company . . . our company."

"Sounds like a worthy strategy," the old man said. "What's the problem?"

"Ha!" I laughed. "Where do I begin? The problem is once again human nature, I guess, territorialism at its worst. Opportunities are lost because different divisions and salespeople within the company are not willing to risk their position with a particular client. There's no communication. Valuable information that could be shared throughout the business is instead held close to the vest. Everyone who is perceived to benefit from the divulgence of such information is considered a threat and held at bay."

"And the company suffers," the old man said.

"Exactly."

"And a relational wall goes up between co-workers, salespeople, even supervisors and staff, that stretches beyond office walls."

"Yes," I said, wondering whether he was reading my mind again. "That's exactly what happens. And I think that's what Tom was getting at. We start to own things too much. We get sidetracked with defending our territory, or at least the territory we think is ours, and we forget about the greater aim of working to strengthen the company. One day we wake up and discover that we are spending far more energy hoarding our clients than working to further the mission of the company."

"Sounds like a full-on breakdown across the board," the old man said.

"It can be," I admitted, "especially when the person who believes his perceived territory is being encroached upon is unwilling to go to the other co-worker and work on a shared resolution. Sadly, that is the case most of the time. Then things really begin to spiral downward. Defensive-minded territorialism takes over. The client's lead salesperson begins to spread information in a negative way throughout the company, making it known that this client is exclusively mine. Now dysfunction is created within the company, and before long you have all-out war, even if it is waged silently—cold shoulders and dispassionate stares in the hallways, an end to friendly chatter in the parking lot. It's as though one employee has identified a fellow worker as the enemy, wordlessly proclaiming, 'You no longer like me, and so I no longer like you, and that's just fine. We'll keep working here in the same company, in the same building, but let's agree to keep our distance, and, oh by the way, please keep your hands off my client!'"

"Wow," the old man said. "Sounds like a lot is floating around under the surface."

"Yeah," I said, in a tone of defeat. "And it seems that Tom finally broke through and stumbled upon a secret."

"I've seen it before."

"Seen what?"

"When people sense the imminence of death, certain things become much clearer to them. There is a mental review of one's life, a greater willingness to be deeply honest with oneself. I think Tom was at that point in his life's journey."

"So you agree with Tom then?" I asked, "that it's best not to 'own it,' not to become too possessive of one's achievements—too, well, territorial?"

"Yes, I agree completely," he said, "but there's something else. *Those who champion an end to division will inherit a place among royalty.*"

"That sounds beautiful," I responded, "but what does it mean?"

"Legacy Virtue number seven—*Peacemaking.*"

I suddenly slipped forward and began to fall off the bench. The old man reached out to steady me before I regained my balance.

"What is it, Jack? What's the matter?"

Still catching my breath. I replied, "It's Tom. He talked about the same thing. He talked about peace. The coincidence in your language startled me."

The old man laughed. "Well," he said, "as I was just saying, Tom was seeing things more clearly. He was focused on what is truly important. He was making peace within himself and, simultaneously, was recognizing the significance of peace in general."

"So how exactly does peacemaking overcome the vice of territorialism?" I asked.

"Peacemaking takes courage," he said, "but the pay-off in countering the negative effects of territorialism can be immediate and lasting. Peacemakers have to be willing to risk vulnerability in an effort to confront problems and work on resolutions. Unfortunately, as you have seen firsthand, territorialism is the standard of the day, whereas peacemaking is somewhat rare. Peacemaking takes time, energy, and effort. It can't be entered into lightly or half-heartedly. Those around you who represent the warring sides of a certain conflict will sense whether or not you are really committed to seeing a situation through to its resolution. If not, they'll eat you up or work behind your back to continue defending their territory. As a leader, you have to make it clear that working toward peace, both relationally and professionally, is going to be the rule, not the exception. But once you establish that platform as foundational to your business, you will begin to see dysfunctionality miraculously vanish."

"Break it down for me. How does the virtue of peacemaking play out one-on-one?"

"Peacemakers make it a habit not to throw others under the bus. Instead, they seek full understanding and work to diffuse potentially explosive situations. They put their egos aside for the greater good of the enterprise and go directly to the person on the other side of the relational divide. However counterintuitive it may seem, the peacemaker expresses how he or she feels, listens to the other person, and opens his or her mind to a response that may clarify why the person is acting as he did. In some cases this kind of honest, direct attempt at understanding might resolve the situation altogether."

"And if not?" I asked.

"If not, then perhaps the seeds of reconciliation are sown and true resolution unfolds over a period of time. All parties have to be open to some level of patience in the process. Initially, when situations of territorialism heat up, it's human nature to approach them somewhat emotionally charged. Again, however right or wrong, it's normal to become defensive. But when we adopt a spirit of peace, having first examined ourselves and admitted some level of responsibility, something begins to change. Diplomacy and grace kick in, and we begin to see the other side's perspective for what it really is, which in most cases has more to do with a fear of losing something he or she has created, as you mentioned earlier. Once a person realizes that it's not your intent to take something away but instead bring greater prosperity to your business as a whole, you would be amazed how mindsets can shift. All of a sudden, instead of one individual's defending what he or she has worked hard for, you have a team focused on maximizing the full potential of a client or project."

"It sounds as though it takes a lot of vulnerability to engage in peace-making," I said, "a lot of humility."

Suddenly I remembered the lesson the old man had demonstrated for me outside his island cottage. I could see that he was thinking the same thing. "The stones," I said. "Humility, now peacemaking, one in need of the other and building upon themselves."

He smiled back at me. "It's really not that complicated if you think about it. There's a wonderful simplicity to how the Great 8 work together."

After a few moments of silence I said, "It's sad," my mind drifting back to those last moments at Tom's bedside the morning before he died.

"How so?" the old man asked.

"That it takes a man's reaching the end of his days before he uncovers some of life's secrets that would have enriched his life had he only un-earthed them years earlier."

"Don't you see, Jack? That was Tom's gift to you. He could have spent his last moments lamenting things left undone, expressing regrets or sounding bitter, but instead he shared his revelations while nearing the ultimate threshold. He divulged the secrets he had uncovered to spare you some of the frustrations and roadblocks he had come up against. He shared this gift so that *you* would not find yourself in a similar position at the end of your life before coming to these same conclusions. He wanted you to have the chance to live the rest of your life in the light of these truths."

All I could do was listen and nod in agreement.

"And there is one other thing," he said. "I don't think that Tom shared what he did *only* for you."

"What do you mean?"

"I believe that if Tom were sitting here between us on this bench, he would tell you not to keep these revelations to yourself but rather to live them out and pass them on—to Katherine, your children, grandchildren, those you work with, clients, even strangers on the street."

I too felt in my soul that Tom had been trying to impart something to me in the hospital, to empower me for things to come. Some of his final words flooded my memory: "Give things away. Don't let them own you.

Love Katherine. Love your kids, and love their kids." And then his response after I shared the idea of *praus* with him: "if I have lived a *praus* life, then I am passing the torch to you. My race is now your race. You carry the mantle for both of us."

Suddenly the memory of Tom's charge that I pass these things on to others directed my mind to Katherine and Beth and all those people gathered at the reception. I needed to be there. I needed to walk among them and tell them what a wonderful man Tom had been. I needed to offer my presence as a way of honoring him, as a testimony to the deep friendship we had shared.

"I need to go," I said abruptly to the old man.

Now it was his turn to nod. "Of course you do," he said. "I've kept you too long."

We both stood.

"You should come too," I said, at the same time wondering how in the world I would explain his presence to Katherine.

"Oh, that would be nice, but I really must get going. I've got some things to do and a few people to see before I head home."

"Thanks for everything," I said. Then I remembered the list. "We didn't get to number eight, my last vice and your corresponding virtue."

"In time," the old man responded, nodding toward the crinkled paper with the vices scribbled on it. "You keep that. Don't worry, I know how to reach you."

"Okay," I said, "but if it suits your schedule, don't stay away too long."

He clasped my hand and gave me that fatherly smile again. Somehow I knew that I would see him again and that the timing would be perfect.

We parted company, I walked toward the reception on the far side of the church property. Instinctively I looked back to see in which direction the old man was headed, but he was nowhere in sight.

13

Frozen Again

*At dawn the men emerged from what shelter was still stand-
ing and fanned out like ghosts among the ruined camp. Slowly
they made their way among the devastation, shaking their heads
and picking through the debris, pulling out certain items here
and there that might prove useful for the journey ahead. The
soldier-rider stood looking blankly at the fallen stables. He stepped
about the wreckage looking at the dead horses where they lay,
preparing himself for that moment when he would come upon the
great stallion. But his horse was nowhere to be found. Surely the
mighty destrier had not fled with the others, he thought. He was
too noble for such an act of desertion. But where then had he gone?
Suddenly the soldier-rider whirled and ran toward the clearing at
the edge of camp. In a minute's time he reached what remained of
the makeshift corral. Every rail and post had been flattened by the
storm's fury save one. On the far side of the clearing a single post
remained, and there stood the great stallion. He lowered his head
as the man crossed the distance between them. When the soldier-
rider reached for the reins and stroked that long-boned cheek, the
horse neighed and gave a soft snort.*

*"You're still in one piece, boy," said the soldier-rider, "just as
I knew you would be. A true war horse you are."*

They stood that way for some time, horse and rider, seeming to find comfort in each other's presence, knowing that they had both survived the first of many long, difficult nights together.

I was stuck again.

Since Tom's funeral. I had taken a few days off from work, intending to give myself some concentrated time to grieve, but then I planned to jump back into life with both feet. I knew that the heavy sadness of Tom's passing would linger for months, if not years, but I imagined that my newfound convictions about the Legacy Virtues and my determination to implement the Great 8 at work would provide me with a burst of energy to offset the blow of losing my best friend and business partner. If nothing else, I thought, I owed this to Tom. He more than anyone would want me to get back out there, to forge ahead, to face the future with strength and fortitude, spurred on by his final words to me. Instead, I found myself lying in bed longer than I intended in the mornings. My normal appetite had abandoned me; I felt disconnected from Katherine. In many ways, though I hated to admit it, things felt much as they had been before our vacation. This was troubling to me. Surely, I reflected, those magical days on the old man's hidden island and all that I absorbed there had not been in vain? But something I couldn't name was plaguing me. I felt paralyzed.

These were my feelings when I awoke late on the Friday after Tom died, dressed hastily, pulled on a ball cap, and announced to Katherine that I was heading out to Starbucks. Without a word she nodded to me over her coffee cup at the kitchen table. As always, she knew that I needed some alone time.

Just before I left the house I had the urge to locate my weathered page of vices. I found the list stuffed in the inside pocket of the suit coat I had worn to Tom's funeral. I shoved the page into the pocket of my blue jeans and headed out the door.

At the coffee shop I ordered a double Americano and then was faced with an early-morning dilemma. The corner table where Tom and I had customarily sat was surprisingly unoccupied. It felt vaguely sacred to me now that Tom was gone. Would I somehow be tarnishing his memory and our times together there if I now sat alone? I decided that this concern was silly. If anything I'd be honoring Tom by sitting at our table, so I settled on a compromise. I walked to the table, pulled out two chairs as if Tom would soon join me, and sat down opposite the ghost chair. I sat down and sipped my coffee. After a few moments I became aware of moisture around my eyes.

The feeling was almost too much to bear. I started to reach for my coffee when my cell phone rang. I pulled it from my pocket and studied the incoming number displayed on the screen. I didn't recognize it, but it could be an international call. Who would be calling me from overseas? Probably a telemarketer from Mumbai or Manila, I thought, and just as I was about to hit the decline option another possibility crossed my mind. Could it be the old man? I didn't recall ever having given him my number. No, I thought, it couldn't be possible. then, in the very next moment, I was so sure that it was in fact him that when I finally answered I said hello with a clear inflection of certainty. It was almost as if I had been waiting for his call.

"How are you?" the old man asked. The connection was remarkably strong.

"Not so good," I answered. "I feel a bit, well, frozen."

"Frozen?" the old man repeated.

"Yeah, frozen. " I then told him about my uninspired mornings and inability to get back to work. I confessed my lack of motivation to go about the business of honoring Tom's memory and pursuing his final commission. "I desperately want to get back out there and put into practice all of those things, "I said, ."but I just can't. Something is holding me back. I don't know what it is exactly. I can't really put a finger on it. Can't seem to give it a name."

"I see," said the old man after a lull. I wondered whether the phone connection had been lost.

"Jack?" he said, breaking the silence. He was still there,

"Yes?"

"Do you by any chance have your list with you now? The vices?"

"Actually, yes, I do. It's amazing that you would even ask. I grabbed it at the very last minute before leaving the house, almost as an afterthought."

The old man chuckled. "Well, I've been told once or twice that my timing is exceptional."

I unfolded the list. "Okay," I said. "I have it in front of me."

"The last entry," he said. "Tell me what it is. Maybe it will help us to figure out what's causing you to feel so paralyzed."

When my eyes scanned down the page to to where number eight should have been, I was dumbfounded.. Considering how many times I had amended the list, I had failed to catch the final omission. I explained all of this to the old man.

"Hmm," he murmured before adding, "Well, let's just both agree that there must have been a reason, some mysterious explanation that we may or may not later understand."

"Agreed," I said. "I can accept that. But what to do about number eight?"

The old man didn't hesitate.

"Tell me first," he said, "how would you describe what's going on inside of you now? What does it *feel* is taking place that's holding you back from moving forward? If you can't name it, can you at least describe it to me?"

I took a few moments to think hard about the old man's question. I looked around the Starbucks, as if someone might be available to help me articulate what was causing me to feel so stuck. It was getting close to mid-morning, not exactly a busy time at the coffee shop, what with the morning rush long over and the lunch crowd still not on hand. I took another sip of my Americano.

"I think so, " I finally answered. "At least I can try."

"Take your time. I've got all day."

"To be completely honest," I said, "I think much of it is rooted in insecurity. I know that everything you shared with me this past week is grounded in sound principles, yet a part of me is worried about what might happen if I do in fact commit to applying the Legacy Virtues in my everyday life."

The old man was silent on the other end of the line. I accepted that as his invitation to continue.

"It's almost as if a voice is telling me to play it cool and just accept the status quo. Some force is trying to convince me that if I do otherwise, if I try to live up to these virtues you've shared with me, that I'll face opposition, maybe ridicule, and possibly commit professional suicide. I can almost envision some cynic suggesting that if I push forward with this new mindset I'll have only myself to blame when the response is not what I'd hoped for."

"Jack," the old man said, his fatherly tone returning, "I can't tell you that the road ahead will be a smooth one. In fact, there is a lot of truth in those words that you seem to be hearing. If you decide to live your life based on the Great 8, there is little doubt that you *will* face some opposition, perhaps some ridicule and pushback. In essence, you will be making a stand, championing newfound convictions, and more times than not such a way of living does invite a certain level of criticism, possibly even outright persecution. The road you are thinking of heading down is in fact a narrow one. But it's the right road Jack, and I think you know that. I think that's part of the reason you are feeling so paralyzed."

"I'm worried, though," I said, "that I won't have the gumption to hang in there when things get rough, that I'll give in to the pushback, that I'll wilt under the pressure and make compromises. I've done that over the years, and I don't want to do that anymore. I don't want to live that way any longer, not at work, not at home, not in any area of my life."

"It's natural to feel this way, Jack. Change is always hard, especially at this stage in your life, especially when you are in a position of leadership. It sounds like you are doing a lot of deep reflection, and your determination not to repeat certain patterns from your past is simultaneously keeping you from charting a new course."

"So I'm right then?" I jumped ahead to what seemed an obvious conclusion. "The last vice on my list should be insecurity? That's my number eight?"

"I don't think so," the old man replied.

"But you just agreed that my fear of not being able to remain true to these new convictions is what might be keeping me from moving forward."

"Aha!" the old man half yelled through the phone. "You just said the word."

"What word?"

"There is something lying deeper than your insecurity, a root of the problem plaguing you, and you just identified it."

I thought back over my last statement. What had I said exactly? I merely pointed out that he seemed to be agreeing with me that my insecurities, rooted in some kind of fear, were most likely ... wait ... I forced my mind to stop and retrace a few steps. "You mean," I took a guess, "*fear*?"

"Exactly."

"So," I said slowly, thinking this through as I asked the question. "You're saying then that whatever makes a child reluctant to let his parent shut off the bedroom light at night is the same thing haunting me these last few days? Pure, unadulterated fear?"

"That's precisely what I'm proposing," came his answer.

It wasn't long until I knew he was absolutely correct. Fear was launching sorties against my normally confident and self-assured nature. Maybe the fact that it seemed such an elementary concept had allowed it to escape me for so long, but now that the old man had led me to this revelation, there was no denying that the culprit was indeed fear. I confessed as much to the old man.

"You see, Jack, your fear of what might happen in the future if you really commit to living under a new set of virtues is causing you to dwell on perceived personal limitations. Instead of resting on the knowledge of what you are in fact capable of, you're doubting yourself. Fear is allowing the uncharted territory that lies just ahead of you to paralyze your better judgment."

"I keep thinking about the risks," I said. "I think about certain people, clients I know, business partners who don't see things the same way Tom did. I know that many of them are going to think I've lost my way, and the criticism they will no doubt level at me is affecting me even now. It's as though I'm visualizing failure, whereas in the past allowing my mind to anticipate success often spurred me on."

There was silence on the other of the line. "Are you there?" I asked.

"Yes," came his reply. "Still here."

"I must sound pretty pathetic," I said. "You're probably thinking that all the time we spent together was a waste."

"That has never once crossed my mind," the old man said, "not before and not now. But I do think you're having a bit of a pity party, and it might be time to end the festivities."

I accepted his metaphor and ran with it. "I'm ready," I said. "Ready to turn out the lights, put away the party favors, shut down the hall, and move on. But therein lies the quintessential question. How? What must I do to chart a course for overcoming my fear?"

"*The one who endures suffering today,*" he said, "*standing firm for that which is virtuous, will tomorrow savor the lasting reward of a life well lived.*"

I waited, as I had so many times before, for the old man to dissect this new idea for me. He didn't disappoint. I guess that he knew me too well by now.

"You can't be swayed by the immediate, Jack, by that which is temporal. You have to envision the road ahead. I'm not saying, 'Don't live in the present moment,' as some might be prone to deduce from this principle. Instead, I'm saying that how you live today and the changes you are willing to undertake, even with all the associated risks, will forever affect your circumstances far into your future. And, for that matter, far into your children's future, your grandchildren's future, and the future of your business—everything and everyone your life touches. I'm talking about your *legacy*, Jack. Our natural default mode is to choose the easy way, to focus on the immediate, but the challenge you must embrace if you want to blaze a new path is to think beyond today. That, my dear friend, *is* and *will be* your legacy."

"Okay", I said, a tone of both agreement and skepticism in my voice. "But how then? How do I trade the temporality of today for the permanence of tomorrow? How do I find the strength and impetus to step out on that proverbial limb that seems to be stretching out before me?"

"I can't tell you now," the old man said.

My heart dropped. "What?" I replied, a bit dumbfounded, feeling almost as if I'd been set up. "Why not?"

"Not over the phone. I need to see you in person to make clear the final virtue. You will just have to trust me on this."

"Okay," I said, not that I had any choice in the matter. "I guess that I can make my way back to the island. It's not as though I'm being very productive around here right now anyway. I need to square it away with Katherine and then. . . ."

"No," he replied, cutting me off. "Not here. Somewhere else."

I waited for him to disclose a location.

"I'll send you the address. It's not so far away from where you are now. Meet me there tomorrow. I'll let you know what time."

"Okay," I said, somewhat perplexed at the apparent need for mystery in the matter. "When will you let me know? How?"

"After we hang up," he said. "I'll text you."

I found this a little comical. "You know how to text?"

I waited for him to laugh, but once more the line was silent. I looked down. This time the call had indeed come to an end. Had he hung up on me, I wondered, or had the call simply been dropped? I was just about to try to return the call when my phone gave a slight buzz, signaling an incoming text. I opened my messages and saw that it was from the same number. It was his text. He asked me to meet him at midnight at the end of the following day. Why such an odd time, I wondered? This was followed by a street, building, and suite number. And then, finally, the city where he wanted the rendezvous to take place.

Well, at least it was a location with which I was pretty familiar. Still, I would need a plane ticket, a hotel for the night, and possibly a rental car. I closed the old man's text and began a search on my cell phone's Internet browser for airline tickets. I found a travel site and typed in the city's name under destination—Chicago.

14

Chicago

Within a few hours another regiment arrived on horses with pack mules in tow. Crossing the plain at the time of the storm, they had managed to make it to the far foothills and waited out the weather in caves, losing no men and no horses or supplies. Now they double-packed the mules. Riders rode two to a horse, and a dozen more men prepared to leave on foot. Just after noon the entire company was gathered at the edge of camp. The horses nervously pawed the dirt, and the pack mules whinnied under their extra burdens.

"How long?" said one soldier to a captain from the fresh regiment.

"A day, two at most," he answered, spitting on the ground and looking off into the distance. "Two more moons, and we'll be in the thick of this thing." The contingent shuffled and slouched, drifting closer together, sensing imminent departure. They were waiting for something, a signal of some sort, a decisive directive that the moment of exodus had arrived.

The soldier-rider sat atop the great stallion and eased him out around the edge of the company. They took their place in front of the newly formed regiment, pausing for just a moment as the soldier-rider exchanged knowing glances with his superiors. The strength and resolve of the stallion were clear.

"Courage boy," the man whispered. "The time has come. Show them what you're made of. Show them your courage."

And with that the soldier-rider sat erect, glanced out over the contingent, lifted the reins, and pushed the heels of his boots firmly into the horse's flanks. Without hesitation the steed lifted his head, fixed his eyes on the low hills in the distance, and began to lead them toward battle.

I got lucky and found one of those last-minute supersaver tickets into Chicago. I knew that it was going to be a bit tougher to explain to Katherine than my need for some solo time at the local Starbucks, but I relied on the old man's words, "You are just going to have to trust me on this." When I broached the matter to her, my sweet and understanding Katherine dropped her eyes, told me she loved me even if I didn't make sense sometimes, and then gave me her blessing.

"It will be a very quick trip," I assured her, "just up and back. I return here tomorrow around noon and will be back home shortly after."

I had hastily packed an overnight bag, which Katherine handed to me as I headed out the door.

"I added a few things," she said. "I know it's spring here, but it's still late winter in Chicago. It's forecasted to dip into the 30s up there tonight. I threw in your heavy fleece jacket, a wool cap, and a scarf, just in case."

I kissed my thoughtful wife and told her I'd see her tomorrow.

Traffic was light on my way to the Atlanta airport, a rarity that I viewed as an omen that good things awaited me in the Windy City. Navigating the airport was also relatively easy, never a given at Hartsfield-Jackson International. The flight was about half full, and I had plenty of room to stretch my legs and rest my arms. It was mid-afternoon, and I had planned to squeeze in a short nap on the plane, but instead I found myself reviewing all that had happened to me over the course of the past week. Before long I had a notebook spread out on the tray table in front of me. My mind quickly drifted to the vices and the corresponding Legacy Virtues. I found myself jotting them down from memory.

Egotism/Humility. That of course was the day I met the old man for the first time. I remembered the shock at seeing my aged self in his facial features. I also recalled how, once that initial shock wore off, he challenged me to summarize all of life's major vices in one short list.

Busyness/Empathy. We discussed these topics the morning I found him high on the bluff overlooking the ocean. I remembered how at that moment I felt as far removed from busyness as any time I could remember in my adult life. I could hear again his explanation that going up there on a regular basis gave him balance and allowed him to empathize with others.

Distraction/Attentiveness. I could see the old man walking down the hillside in front of me and disappearing from view before I rounded a corner to find that he had fallen. Then back at the cottage we waded into our discussion of the next vice and virtue. His fall, however unfortunate, provided a perfect example of the vice of distraction and a template for considering the steadying virtue of attentiveness.

Greed/Accountability. That was the night the old man showed up unannounced on the main island. I recalled the surprise encounter on the dance floor, the effect of his charm on Katherine, and afterwards our time sitting by the ocean's edge sipping wine and dissecting the vice of greed. He and I had marveled at the stars overhead and agreed that the practice of intentional accountability could help someone to maintain ethical standards.

Anger/Acceptance. When we fished together, I shared with him my experiences of seeing so much deeply rooted anger in the business world and all the ways it manifests itself. He listened and then countered with the virtue of acceptance. I could still recite verbatim his claim that "compassion in the form of acceptance is the strongest defense against the vice of anger."

Dishonesty/Integrity. After dining on freshly caught mahi-mahi, we discussed the all too common vice of dishonesty, the only one he maintained that was ingrained in the human psyche from birth onwards. The old man proposed that the willingness to be deceptive was a desperate act of self-preservation. It was after he introduced the accompanying virtue of integrity that he took me over to the cairn of eight large stones to demonstrate how the virtues worked in concert together.

Territorialism/Peacemaking. During our discussion in the park immediately after Tom's funeral, I had proposed that over time many slip into an obsession with defending whatever they have "built" up over the years, perhaps nowhere more than in the corporate world, whether that meant reputation, portfolio, or perceived accomplishments. The old man asserted that the only real way to break down that defense was through peacemaking. We both agreed that this virtue was apparent in Tom's final words.

Fear. Less than twenty-four hours ago the old man had identified the last vice. It was pulling me down into an abyss of paralysis and keeping me from launching into a new world, a new way of thinking and acting, based on the Legacy Virtues. They, I knew, held the hope for my future, both as a businessman and as a human being.

I must have dwelt on these thoughts much longer than I realized because not long after I finished writing them down the flight attendant announced that we had begun our initial descent into the Chicago area. There was a late-season dusting of snow on the ground, and as we taxied toward the terminal I found myself shivering in anticipation of the cold temperatures outside. The old man's island seemed a world away.

I retrieved my rental car and within an hour had checked into my hotel for the night, a national chain not far from the address the old man had given me. I ate a light dinner and then went back to my room and lay down for the nap I had intended to take on the plane. It was only eight o'clock, still four hours before I was to meet the old man. Midnight, he had indicated in his text. What an odd time, I thought again. Why so late? With the television on some mindless channel, I stretched out on the hotel bed, and before I knew it I was in a deep sleep.

I dreamed. It was a disjointed dream, bits and pieces of the past few weeks all jumbled together. I saw the resort island again, Katherine and I dancing by the shore. Then I was out on the water alone in a kayak. It was nighttime. I seemed to be waiting for the storm that would send me through to the other side, but instead of swirling winds and dark clouds the night was eerily silent, the sky overhead rife with stars, stars brighter and clearer than any I could remember. I sat perfectly still, the paddle laid across my lap, the water rising and falling ever so slightly, the ends of the paddle dipping in and out of the ocean's filmy surface. I just stared upward, marveling at the celestial tapestry.

Then the scene changed, and I was running headlong through the woods along the path to the old man's cottage, guided only by the full moonlight. When I finally burst out of the woods and into a clearing, I came to a jolting stop, staring in disbelief across the meadow. The cottage was nowhere to be found! In fact, I saw no trace that it had ever existed. Even the grass in the meadow seemed undisturbed, as if it had always been just what it appeared to be now—an empty expanse in the middle of an island forest. I bent over panting, my hands resting on my knees, trying to catch my breath.

Suddenly I felt a presence behind me. Then I heard something, twigs breaking beneath someone's footsteps. Slowly I turned around and shuddered as a figure emerged from the wooded path. Hoping that it was the old man, I peered into the darkness trying to make out the face. The figure stepped into the clearing and walked slowly in my direction. I braced myself, ready to defend myself if the situation demanded it. The figure walked right up to me until we were separated by a mere two or three paces. The body *appeared* to be that of the old man, and I imagined that I would next recognize his face, yet as his features become more distinct I recoiled and gasped.

There before me was the same face I had encountered the last time I was in Chicago. It was Jerry. Jerry McGuire.

———

I awoke with a jolt. Rubbing my eyes, I glanced at the bedside clock and saw that it was nearly midnight. I must have been more tired than I realized. There was no time to reflect on the dream, no time even to shower. I threw some water on my face, donned my fleece jacket, grabbed the wool cap Katherine had packed for me, and quickly headed out of the hotel. The late March air was chilly, and I pulled the cap down tightly over my head and zipped the jacket all the way up. In the rental car I plugged the address the old man had sent me into the car's GPS system and rushed out of the hotel's parking facility.

Given the late hour, the traffic was light. I followed the verbal directions of the automated guide, encountered a few red lights, wound further into the heart of the city, and before I knew it arrived in front of a large conference hall on a side street just off Michigan Avenue. A few taxis were lined up about a half block down the road, but otherwise the area was noticeably quiet. Suddenly I had an overwhelming sense that *I knew this place*. At first I wasn't sure how, but then I looked up at the facade of the building and instantly knew exactly where I was. No wonder I had dreamed about Jerry McGuire. The address the old man had given me was that of the same conference hall where Tom and I had attended that fateful business seminar only a few weeks earlier.

I parked the car, stepped out into the crisp Chicago night, locked the doors with the remote, and scanned the front of the building. Surely it was locked at this hour, but perhaps that didn't matter to the old man. I had learned by now that he had his ways. Looking north and then south along the street and finding no one watching, I walked up to the building's large glass doors. Even if by some miraculous circumstance the doors were unlocked, I had no doubt that the building was equipped with security systems. My entry would be announced via some internal alarm system as well as on a closed-circuit monitor somewhere else in the city. I was unsure of what to do next. I started to turn back toward the car, thinking that I should wait inside it until my next step became clear, when my cell phone vibrated. I dug it out of my pocket and studied the screen. The text message came from the same number the old man had used yesterday. There were just two words: "Come inside."

I studied the message. Though it wasn't written in the text, I could almost hear two other words trailing those staring up at me: "*Trust me*." How many times had he said this to me over the course of our friendship? And every time I'd trusted him things had turned out precisely as he predicted. With that thought in my head, I approached the large glass doors, placed my hands on the oversized brass handles, and pushed.

With little effort the door swung open. There was no blaring alarm announcing a security breach. Gingerly I stepped into the large foyer and eased the door closed behind me. The foyer was dark, but the street lamps outside offered just enough light that I could see two staircases on either side of the reception area. I remember that they both led up to the second level and the main meeting hall where I had listened in frustration to the seminar speaker as he rambled on in his narcissistic way.

I climbed one of the staircases, crossed the narrow carpeted hallway, and entered the auditorium. The room, filled from top to bottom with theatre-style seats, was bathed in a half darkness. Floor lights running down the aisles and the multiple exit signs around the auditorium showed that all the seats were empty and that I was alone in the great hall.

Then the quiet was broken by a strangely familiar voice over the audio system. It was not the old man's voice. I had heard it before, recently in fact, but couldn't quite place it.

"Have a seat, Jack," said the voice.

Walking slowly so as not to stumble in the half light, I made my way about midway down one of the aisles and slipped into a row where I sat down in one of the comfortable seats. I waited.

I heard the clicking sound of footsteps and could see someone walking out from the left side of the stage. The light was too low to make out the face, so I studied the movements of the body as the male figure walked to the center of the platform. Was it the old man? Suddenly a stage light came on, and I saw exactly who it was. Now I realized that the voice matched the face. They were the same from my earlier dream, which now seemed to have been a premonition. It was Jerry McGuire! He stood at center stage and looked directly at me.

"Life," he said, his voice seeming to boom across the space between us. "Is made up of defining moments—landmarks, epiphanies, corners turned, paths taken and paths *not* taken. In those moments, Jack, if we listen care-fully enough, we can hear voices of truth. Most times we don't know ex-actly where they come from, but that doesn't diminish the significance they play in our lives. We can't be so concerned with where or how those voices come to us that we miss the meaning behind them."

Jerry took a few steps forward, almost to the edge of the stage. He stared at me. His eyes locked with mine. If he weren't so real standing there before me, his voice so clear, I would have guessed that I was back in the hotel and immersed in my dream.

"This," he continued, "is your moment, Jack. Everything you did be-fore now and everything you'll do from now onward will come back to this point in time. Don't miss it. Listen to your heart. Listen to your con-victions. And most importantly of all. . . ." He paused, and I instinctively leaned forward in my seat. "Demonstrate the same thing you did a few weeks ago when you walked out of this room frustrated and discouraged. Don't settle for the status quo. Don't just accept the shortcomings of the business world and give up. Don't ever give up. Courage, Jack. Have . . . *courage.*"

Then, as deliberately as he had entered, Jerry McGuire turned and left. The clicking of his shoes on the wooden stage faded away, and the light went off. For a moment I was alone again. Suddenly the house lights came up, and I was jolted by the reality that someone was sitting in the seat directly beside me. It was the old man! How long had he been there, I wondered? Had he been beside me throughout Jerry's speech? Wait a minute. The old man claimed to have appeared to me as Jerry the first time I encountered the movie icon. I assumed that he had just done so again.

"Well," he said almost nonchalantly, as if I should not be surprised by his sudden appearance. He was staring ahead at the stage where Jerry had been. "So what do you think?"

"I think you startled me just now," I responded. I had somewhat gotten used to his propensity for materializing at any time, in any fashion, at any place—on the dance floor at the island resort, in the back of the church during Tom's funeral, on the phone at Starbucks—yet finding him there right beside me in the vastness of the empty auditorium with no prior warning, after a soliloquy delivered by the ghost of Jerry McGuire, did make me jump.

"Ha!" he said, reaching over to pat me on the shoulder, apparently amused at his ability still to shock me. "No, I mean about what Jerry said up there. All that dramatic verbiage about defining moments and corners turned, paths taken, and hearing voices. Did any of it resonate with you?"

"All of it," I admitted. "Every single word."

"And did you catch the golden nugget he gave you?"

"What do you mean?" I said, momentarily stumped.

"The opposing force to your eighth vice," he said. "Jerry articulated the final virtue, the counterpoint to fear, the last of the Great 8."

I thought back through Jerry's words in my head. *"Don't miss it,"* he had said. *"Listen to your heart. Listen to your convictions. Don't settle for the status quo. Don't ever give up."* The tape in my head wound to the end, and I was left with only one option. When I repeated it to the old man, I knew immediately that this was the final Legacy Virtue, number eight.

"Courage," I said.

"Yes, courage," the old man affirmed.

"The same thing that enables the little boy to remain in his room," I began, thinking back to the analogy in our last conversation about fear, "and endure the night even though he fears monsters under the bed."

"Exactly, " said the old man. "And on a grander scale the same thing that enabled Tom to face death with such dignity and hope, enough so that he was able to impart those final words of wisdom to his best friend only hours before he passed from this life to the next."

"Courage," I repeated again, letting the concept sink into my brain.

"Courage indeed," said the old man, "but it's important to understand that there are two kinds of courage. One must be able to differentiate between them in order to claim the authentic one."

He had my full attention.

"There is courage couched in bravado," he said. "when someone hypes himself up. He works to convince his psyche that he can push through a certain situation or face a difficult circumstance. The problem is that once the challenge is over, whether or not he survives or succeeds, the virtue fades. This is false courage."

I was following him. Memories flashed in my mind of when, while playing high school and collegiate football, I psyched myself up for a certain opponent, a particular play, or a crucial moment in the game. It usually worked, but I could see the old man's point. In those moments I was summoning a temporary measure of courage. Once the game ended, my sense of confidence typically faded simply because I no longer had need for it. But, of course, life was not a game.

"Real courage, genuine courage," the old man continued, "can only come when one is first willing to be gut-level honest about his or her fears. No one enjoys fear. No one wants to spend any more time than necessary besieged by it, but unless we understand what it is that causes us to be afraid, what brings us trepidation, unless we work again and again to name such beasts, courage will prove fleeting and only situational, leaving us frustrated and, well, afraid."

"So, then, how do we do that? How do we name our fears?"

The old man sighed and turned to look at me. "This is where you might become angry with me," he said.

"How so?"

"Because you're asking me something that I can't tell you. Only you, Jack, can discover and name your fears."

He saw my immediate look of disappointment and put his arm around my shoulder.

"That's the bad news. I can't help you much there. But here's the good news. I *can* give you the key."

"The key?"

"The key to knowing how to understand what causes you fear and anxiety."

"I'm listening."

"Hide nothing from yourself. Be brutally transparent in your self-evaluation, in any part of your life where you desire to see courage triumph over fear. It's an overused cliché, but it fits here perfectly: you have nothing to lose."

"And once I identify my fears, what then?"

"Then you take those fears, you claim them as valid—no point in denying something you know is real—you put them underfoot and bury them. When they try to raise their heads in the future, you wave your finger in protest and stomp on them again. And again. And again."

"It can't be that easy," I said.

"I'm not saying that it will be," he agreed. "Not at all. But I *am* saying that it's possible. When you commit to practicing genuine courage, making it a daily behavior and not just something you summon for temporary situations, over time you will gain the confidence necessary to help you implement the virtues in every area of your life. Sure, there will be some trial and error. At certain times those old fears will rise up from the grave and try to gain a foothold on you, but you keep shoveling dirt on top of them. Eventually they will disappear for good, and you will be wholly free from them."

I remained quiet, ruminating on his words.

"It's one foot in front of the other sometimes," the old man said. "They are some of the hardest steps you will ever take, but you have to take the first one, Jack, in order to set the rest in motion. Living out the virtues instead of succumbing to the vices eventually becomes a natural habit. Facing adversity, whether in the form of a business decision, a personnel issue, a client relationship, a co-worker dynamic, virtually anything, can be done with courage as the chief agent instead of fear."

"One foot in front of the other," I repeated.

"That's right," the old man said. "That's where it starts."

Again followed a few moments of silence while I let his words penetrate.

"Jack, it's like *praus*. It's like the nature of that Greek war horse."

"How so?" I asked.

"Courage places a man on the edge of two very different realities. On the one hand, it marks a deep desire not to give in to something, not to surrender or give up. In war, of course, the ultimate avoidance is death, even though the possibility of death is a constant in battle. At the same time the motivation to demonstrate courage is connected to survival and all that survival means, the opposite of death—namely, life. And the irony, the seeming contradiction, is that in this state of mind a person is displaying the willingness to approach either reality, death or life. A coward runs *from* both death and life. A courageous man, like the war horse, runs *toward* both, hoping of course for the latter. In this way a courageous man is demonstrating the very same obedience as the praus."

"But what if the courage fades?" I asked. "What if I stumble?"

The old man didn't hesitate. "Then call it a day, get up the next morning, and take another step. You commit each day to live your life from the center, from the collective virtues, and then keep stepping in that direction."

We sat in silence together. I could sense the end of our time together drawing ever nearer. I didn't want my time in his presence to end, yet, perhaps as evidence that I was claiming the courage he spoke of, I wanted to rush back home to Katherine and my life in Georgia to begin living from this new center. He sensed it too. He had that way about him.

"You will be fine, Jack," he reassured me. "You have all the tools you need and all the capability in the world. I think you're ready."

We made our way quietly out into the hallway and down the stairs, then through the front doors to the sidewalk. The temperature had dropped another five or ten degrees, and we both shivered as we stood together beneath a canopy of brilliant stars draped over the Chicago skyline. I grabbed the wool cap from my coat pocket and pulled it down tight over my head and ears.

"Will I see you again?" I asked.

He smiled. "Every day. Every time you look in the mirror. And perhaps more clearly as you grow older." His smile widened when he said this.

"I guess I'll have to live with that," I said, only partially comforted by his answer.

"As I said, you'll be fine, Jack. I have a lot of faith in you. I think that you're going to surprise yourself."

I forced a smile, then wrapped my arms around the old man and hugged him. He hugged me back, and we remained that way for a long moment. For a second I thought about my father, who had passed away many years ago. I could not recall the last time we had embraced like this before his death. It felt good; it felt affirming; it felt powerful. It was almost as if the old man was transmitting some of his own strength to my very being.

We broke our embrace and nodded to one another.

"Well then," he said. "Farewell, my friend. Fare well, Jack."

"I will miss you," I blurted out.

"I as well," he replied, "very much so."

Then he turned and, looking up at the star-studded night sky, began to walk away from me. After just a few steps he suddenly stopped and turned back in my direction.

"You see that, Jack?" he called to me. He was pointing to the sky.

"What?" I said.

"The stars. They're the same ones as above my island, the same ones that shine over Atlanta."

I nodded again and smiled at him. He smiled back, gave me a quick and final wave, and then, as unexpectedly as he had entered my life inside that small cabin in the middle of a mysterious island somewhere in the Caribbean, he walked away. A block down Michigan Avenue to the north he stopped, look both ways as if undecided where he was going next, and then, just like that, turned the corner and was gone. I stood there for what seemed like an eternity, long enough that my fingers started to feel slightly frozen, and then crossed the street. I fumbled with the car key for a moment, wiped a tear from my eye, started the engine, and made my way back to the hotel. All the while I drove leaning forward, craning my neck to look up through the car's windshield to study those magnificent stars, not wanting them to fade away.

———

On the plane home the next morning I again found myself staring down at my open notebook, reviewing the list of vices and virtues that I had drafted on the flight to Chicago. The temperature inside the plane felt abnormally cool to me, despite the fact that I was wearing a sweater. I stopped my review long enough to retrieve my fleece jacket from the overhead storage bin and put it on. I raised the zipper nearly to my neck and returned to my notes.

They were all there now, the vices and virtues, save for one. I pulled the pen out of the binder and across from the word *Fear* wrote down the final virtue—*Courage*. My list was complete. I had the Great 8. I stared down at the page.

One foot in front of the other. My mind recalled the old man's words. *Live your life from the center . . . from the collective virtues.* I could hear the inflection in his voice as he delivered those final injunctions. Then I did something without really knowing why. Slowly, but intentionally, I drew a line through each of the vices. One by one they were struck from the page.

Egotism, busyness, distraction. Down they went. *Greed, anger, dishonesty.* Into the abyss. And finally *territorialism* and *fear*.

I knew it wasn't that simple. I knew that they were going to try to haunt me no matter how much I committed myself to burying them forever. But that's when I would pick myself up and do exactly what the old man told me to do. *Keep stepping in that direction*, in the direction of the virtues. And now I took my pen and circled each one. I did so while whispering them to myself.

Humility, empathy, attentiveness. I said them under my breath with measured pace, letting each syllable tumble over my lips. *Accountability* and *acceptance.* I circled and said them with deep conviction, as if willing the meanings of the words into my core. *Integrity, peacemaking,* and finally *courage.*

I stared at the page. I must have been concentrating pretty hard because I missed the announcement about our initial descent and all those standard airline instructions about preparing the cabin for landing. A flight attendant motioned for me to fold up my tray table. I closed the notebook and folded up the collapsible tray, and when I did so my pen fell to the floor. I picked it up and deposited it in the pocket of my fleece jacket. When I reached my hand inside the jacket, though, I found something already there. My fingers curled around the shell necklace. That was strange, I thought. I didn't take this jacket to the tropics, and I didn't recall wearing it until the night before.

Katherine, I immediately thought. She must have found the necklace and put it inside the jacket before packing it in my overnight bag. I opened the shell. The pearl was still there, just as shiny as when I first saw it on the flight home from the island. I touched the gem's surface. It was smooth, slick, cool to the touch. Then I closed the shell, lifted the necklace, and fastened it around my neck, tucking the shell inside my sweater. I rested my hand on where the shell lay nestled and kept it there as the plane descended. Looking out the window, I watched as the city of Atlanta came into view. As I heard the landing gear being lowered, I knew that I was on the threshold of a new season in life.

A million thoughts rushed through my brain and then all coalesced in the same image—the war horse, my new ideal and standard. I wanted to wake each day braced for battle, on guard against the vices and ready to defeat them with their countering virtues. The road would be difficult, no doubt, but I'd have Katherine to hold me accountable as well as the memories of Tom and, of course, the words of the old man.

I fingered the necklace through my clothing, and a smile broke across my face. Just before the plane touched down, I couldn't help but say aloud one word repeatedly: *praus, praus, praus.* I was home.

Postscript

For some readers, perhaps, the cat is already out of the bag. For others here's the deal: the Legacy Virtues or the "Great 8," while transcending any era, culture, or ethnicity, are based on principles expounded in a speech on a hillside in first-century Palestine. The speaker was Jesus of Nazareth, the itinerant Jewish preacher and miracle-worker. Whether or not one believes the ultimate claim of Jesus that he was the human manifestation of God, the wisdom he delivered that day on that hillside holds as much weight today as it did back then. Most of us, regardless of our religious belief or disbelief, will find little argument with the truth of those eight principles, known more formally as the "Beatitudes." They are universally regarded as a framework for how we might best live and work among others.

While their practice requires commitment and at times struggle, it's hard to go wrong when we strive to live up to these standards. Of course, claiming these principles and trying to live by them is much easier said than done, but that is exactly what my friend and *de facto* mentor David Harper has done. My book titled *Praus: A Parable for Winning the War Within* simply builds on his manuscript *The Great 8: A New Paradigm for Leadership*, a practical short work in which David masterfully argued for the Beatitudes' central role in the business world. The "old man" in *Praus* is loosely modeled on David. Likewise, David's wife Anne is the template for my fictitious Katherine. Jack's dear friend and business partner Tom is based on David's colleague Bill Straub, who battled cancer and finally succumbed a few years before *The Great 8* was published. Just as Tom did in the literary realm, Bill fought with courage until his final days and never compromised or stopped championing the call for an ethical approach to business.

Praus is my attempt to expand on David's profound work so that readers might be challenged to consider the power of the biblical virtues, first proclaimed on a hillside in first-century Galilee, and their application to twenty-first-century life. Enumerated below are the virtues matched with the beatitudes from which they derive, along with what I would call a "parallel beatitude" articulated by the "old man."

"Blessed are the poor in spirit, for theirs is the kingdom of heaven."
The treasure of the unassuming is possession, in the end, of that which is of highest value.
Egotism is countermanded by humility.

"Blessed are those who mourn, for they will be comforted."
He who builds a bridge to those around him will become heir to life's richest peace.
Busyness is countermanded by empathy.

"Blessed are the meek, for they will inherit the earth."
Power tamed gives way to mastery of all that surrounds you.
Distraction is countermanded by attentiveness.

"Blessed are those who hunger and thirst for righteousness, for they will be filled."
Seek what is noble and just, resisting the urge toward the vain accumulation of that which is perishable, and your appetite will be quenched by overwhelming abundance.
Greed is countermanded by accountability.

"Blessed are the merciful, for they will be shown mercy."

Twice richer is the one who pours out compassion on others, for he in turn will receive double the dose of the same.

Anger is countermanded by acceptance.

"Blessed are the pure in heart, for they will see God."

The one who sets himself apart, protecting the honor of his core, will gain an audience with the source of all that is good and right.

Dishonesty is countermanded by integrity.

"Blessed are the peacemakers, for they will be called sons of God."

Those who champion an end to division will inherit a place among royalty.

Territorialism is countermanded by peacemaking.

"Blessed are those who are persecuted because of righteousness, for theirs is the kingdom of heaven."

The one who endures suffering today, standing firm for that which is virtuous, will tomorrow savor the lasting reward of a life well lived.

Fear is countermanded by courage.

Collectively the Legacy Virtues stand in stark contrast to their respective vices but are interdependent. Much like those eight stones sitting atop one another outside the old man's island cottage, removing or ignoring one of the virtues can have a crippling effect on the others. Conversely, taken together, the virtues significantly increase the ceiling for success in business, in relationships, and in life. As he explains so well in *The Great 8*, David Harper connects the practicing of the virtues to something he labels "relational capital." David writes, "Relational capital in the business valuation world is a part of the intangible assets of a company—associated with all of the relationships a company has both internally and externally."

Living out the virtues fosters the greatest possible atmosphere for genuine, sincere, healthy, and positive relationships, both within a company and within the client-employee dynamic. Simply put, the more an employee demonstrates the character traits associated with the virtues, the more likely co-workers are to flourish and enjoy coming to work each day, and the more likely clients are to appreciate their relationships to the company.

Conversely, David warns, "Negligence in embracing the virtues *diminishes* relational capital and negatively affects the value of the enterprise in the long run. Not only do the virtues build [positive] relationships, which is good in and of itself," David suggests, but there are also "long term financial implications as well, especially in the area of attracting and retaining the right people to our respective organizations."

When employees take the Great 8 virtues seriously and commit themselves to implementing the virtues both inwardly and outwardly, everyone wins. Clients feel genuinely cared for; sales personnel tend to meet or exceed expectations; and the company as a whole prospers. Not only that but outside the workplace people's lives are often transformed, since these same principles hold true in all interpersonal relationships.

Finally, permit me again to quote that same first-century Nazarene. Before he left the crowd that day on the hillside, he gave them one last caution and accompanying counsel. First the caution:

> Everyone who hears these words of mine and does **not** do them is like a foolish man who built his house on sand. The rain fell, the flood came, and the winds beat against that house and it collapsed; it was utterly destroyed. (Matt. 7:26-27; New English Translation)

His words of warning followed a final nugget of wisdom he offered before resting his voice. In their most basic terms, they were a profound encouragement to be a people who "walk the talk":

> Everyone who hears these words of mine and does them is like a wise man who built his house on rock. The rain fell, the flood came, and the winds beat against that house, but it did not collapse

because it had been founded on rock. (Matt. 7:24-25; New English Translation)

It seems so simple, no matter our belief systems, a lesson we were taught as schoolchildren and yet somehow forgot or chose to ignore as we grew older. *Build your house upon the rock.*

May the Legacy Virtues prove to be the "rock" for you, a solid and true foundation. May you find the courage to face and defeat your personal fears and insecurities, rising up, like that Greek war horse, so that long before your days end you find yourself living a *praus* life.

Hunter Lambeth
Nazareth, Israel
June, 2015

About the Author

Hunter Lambeth grew up in North Carolina and graduated from the University of North Carolina before hitting the proverbial road. He has lived in Mexico, Hawaii, Montana, and Georgia. Most of his adult life has been spent working closely with teens and young adults through the international organization Young Life. For thirteen years Hunter directed Young Life's "Expeditions," a short-term service program that took him repeatedly to Central America, East Africa, and the Caribbean island of Hispaniola.

Hunter, his wife Lauri, and their daughter Haley live and work in Nazareth, Israel, where they encourage youth of all ethnic and religious backgrounds to consider life's deepest and most profound questions, opening doors of needed cross-cultural dialogue.

Made in the USA
Charleston, SC
03 February 2016